SCOTTISH
BODYSNATCHERS

SCOTTISH
BODYSNATCHERS

A Gazetteer

GEOFF HOLDER

ACKNOWLEDGEMENTS

As someone who thinks libraries and museums are treasures beyond measure, I am delighted to thank the following fine institutions: East Lothian Library Services, West Lothian Local History Library, Midlothian Local Studies Library, South Lanarkshire Museums, Dumfries Museums, Scottish Borders Museums, Aberdeenshire Museum Service, and the long-suffering AK Bell Library in Perth. I am deeply grateful to the assistance, knowledge and images supplied by Geoff Bailey, Keeper of Archaeology & Local History at Falkirk Museum; Dalkeith History Society, especially David Smith and Alan Mason; Leslie Thomson; John Arthur of South Leith Parish Church; Cate Ludlow; and Billy Kerr of Irvine (it's amazing who you run into in graveyards). And a tip of the stovepipe hat to Norman Adams, bodysnatching pandit of this parish. As ever, Ségolène Dupuy was the bee's knees and the cat's pyjamas.

This book is one of a series dealing with the strange, mysterious and bizarre. For more information, or to contribute your own story, go to www.geoffholder.co.uk.

This book is dedicated to all those who carry an organ donor card.
See www.organdonation.nhs.uk

First published 2010

The History Press
The Mill, Brimscombe Port
Stroud, Gloucestershire, GL5 2QG
www.thehistorypress.co.uk

© Geoff Holder, 2010

The right of Geoff Holder to be identified as the Author
of this work has been asserted in accordance with the
Copyrights, Designs and Patents Act 1988.

British Library Cataloguing in Publication Data.
A catalogue record for this book is available from the British Library.

ISBN 978 0 7524 5603 4

Typesetting and origination by The History Press
Printed in Great Britain

CONTENTS

INTRODUCTION

> To examine the causes of life, we must first have recourse to death.
>
> Mary Shelley, *Frankenstein*

Imagine you are in a lonely Scottish churchyard on a dark moonless night. By the light of a shaded lantern you and your companions dig into a fresh grave, carefully depositing the earth on a spread-out sheet. By the time you are waist-deep in the hole, it is the hardest physical labour you have ever undertaken; you are soaked with sweat. Six feet down, your spade bangs against wood. A crowbar-like tool is used to break open the upper coffin. If the funeral has been recent and the winter cold, there will be little smell, but if conditions are the opposite you are hit full in the face with the reek of putrefaction. Your companions lower a rope which is placed around the neck, and in a series of jerks the corpse is hauled up to the surface. The death-shroud is stripped off and left in the coffin – after all, a corpse does not belong to anyone but you do not want to be accused of theft of property – and the earth tipped back into the hole. The body is placed into a sack, and your team climb over the graveyard wall to a waiting one-horse carriage. If you are lucky, you arrive at your destination in the city without being shot at by watchmen, pursued by an angry mob, or stopped and arrested at a toll-bar or barricade.

Why would anyone desecrate the dead, subject themselves to such harrowing experiences, and take such risks with their life and liberty? The answer was a mix of necessity and greed.

As the conflict with Napoleonic France expanded into the first true World War, the demand for surgeons within the Army and Navy rocketed. Hundreds of young men flocked to what was universally agreed to be the finest medical training-ground in the English-speaking world – Scotland. And each student needed to dissect at least one corpse in order to be an effective doctor when faced with injured people in real life. Unfortunately, the law in Britain was hopelessly out of date. The only bodies that could be legitimately obtained were of executed murderers. You could be hanged for dozens of offences, but only murder attracted the additional penalty of post-mortem dissection. Even in an especially violent year, the number of murderers making it to the anatomy classes was just a handful. Meanwhile, hundreds of students could not qualify as doctors unless they had dissected a body.

The answer was obvious, if unpalatable – break the law and go against common decency, and steal freshly-buried bodies. Bodysnatching commenced in Edinburgh, home of the best and largest medical school, but then spread to the other two Scottish centres for anatomical education, Glasgow and Aberdeen. At a conservative estimate, perhaps 800 cadavers a year were required (Edinburgh alone had 500 medical students). And so came the rise of the bodysnatchers, the resurrectionists, the sack-'em-up men, the susie-lifters, the graveyard ghouls.

WHO WERE THE SNATCHERS?

1. The Medical Students

At the start, the snatchers were the primary consumers – medical students (and sometimes even their professors). The motive was obvious – each student needed at least one body to complete their studies – although sometimes the execution was poor, with amateurish mistakes. Some students only 'lifted' a body once, but poorer ones found they could pay for their tuition fees by selling a stock of cadavers to their colleagues. Sometimes, established country doctors, approached by fellow alumni, acted as informants for the big-city boys.

2. The Gravediggers
Sextons were poorly paid, so were easily bribed. Sometimes they merely informed the resurrectionists about a fresh burial, while on other occasions they participated in the lifting. Others deliberately dug very shallow graves, or even spirited the body out of the coffin before the burial. When a grave was found violated, suspicion frequently fell on the gravedigger, often justifiably.

3. The Professionals
After around 1819, competition between surgeons in Edinburgh raised prices for corpses, so the profits inevitably attracted experienced criminals, sometimes referred to as 'the scum of the earth'. Edinburgh had at least three professional bodysnatching gangs, while Glasgow, where prices were lower, had perhaps one. Aberdeen, cheaper and smaller, had no major gang, more a number of part-time professionals who lifted on the side.

Having cash-conscious criminals on the books made for some colourful episodes. Two sold a body to Dr Lizars, then stole it back from his dissecting room and flogged it to Dr Knox, making a tidy £25 in total. In 1828 a woman showed a letter to a medical man that stated she would shortly be receiving 'a very valuable box from the country'. £2 10s was paid in advance for the presumed contents – which proved to be stones packed in straw (the swindlers received 60 days' detention in the Bridewell). And Robert Liston, a spectacularly adventurous Edinburgh surgeon who regarded bodysnatching as an extension of his sporting prowess, even hired Ben Crouch, the ex-leader of a London bodysnatching gang, as a tutor!

BURKE AND HARE, AT YOUR SERVICE
It is due to Burke and Hare that everyone has heard of bodysnatching. It is ironic, then, that they were not bodysnatchers. That is, they never dug up a body from a grave – they were not resurrection-men. They were, in fact, serial killers – and the most prolific serial-killing duo in British history. Between November 1827 and October 1828 they murdered sixteen people in cold blood and sold the corpses to the Edinburgh anatomists.

Their first sale was not a murder and is not included in the total of sixteen. An elderly tenant died of illness in William Hare's cheap lodging-house, leaving an unpaid debt for rent. Hare and his friend William Burke opened the coffin and took the corpse to Surgeons' Square where, after some bumbling resulting from their inexperience, they received the fabulous sum of £7 10s. Had lightbulbs been invented by this time, they would have gone off above their heads. Cadavers clearly equalled cash, and lots of it. Hare's lodging-

A typical sensational take on the Burke and Hare murders, taken from the Victorian true-crime magazine *Famous Crimes.*

Famous Crimes had no doubt that Mrs Burke and Mrs Hare were complicit in the murders.

house business in West Port meant people were always coming and going, so why not cut out the risky and laborious graverobbing shenanigans and go straight to the source? People, they reasoned, were basically walking skin-bags of valuable organs and bones, a natural resource just begging to be harvested by the enterprising entrepreneur. And, of course, many of the itinerant poor attracted to the bottom-of-the-market lodgings would not be missed – a proposition proven by events, for even today the names of six of their victims remain unknown while a further two are recorded only by their first names. The average price paid per corpse was £10, which largely went on drink. The preferred murder method was suffocation, which guaranteed an unmarked corpse. Following the trial the word 'burking', meaning to kill by suffocation or strangulation, entered the English language.

William Burke was thirty-six years old in 1828, William Hare twenty-one. Although each murdered one person on their own, they were effectively a classic example of a toxic couple, where each participant needed the other in order to kill effectively. They were aided and abetted in their crimes by thirty-one-year-old Margaret Logue, the mother of Hare's infant child, and thirty-three-year-old Helen McDougal, Burke's wife or partner of ten years, and the only one of the quartet not from Ireland. In the mid-1820s perhaps five per cent of the population of Edinburgh was Irish. The men had separately pursued low-paid labouring and semi-skilled occupations, until Burke and Helen landed up at the lodging-house in Tanner's Close owned by Margaret and run by Hare. Margaret always made sure she got a £1 'landlady's fee' for every murder the men committed on her premises. (Tanner's Close and the surrounding slums were demolished in 1902, its footprint now obscured by Argyll House.)

As the killings proceeded the pair became reckless, even foolhardy, and they were eventually caught after some elementary mistakes from the *Big Book of What Not To Do If You Are A Serial Killer*. The trial lasted all day and all night on Christmas Eve. Due to the lack of compelling evidence, a deal was struck. The prosecution's star witness was William Hare, granted immunity from prosecution if he testified against his former partners-in-crime. Helen McDougal was prosecuted but not convicted. Burke was found guilty and hanged before a vast crowd on 28 January 1829. Hare, his wife and Helen McDougal were released, and their post-trial adventures percolate through this book. The primary recipient of the cadavers, the distinguished teacher of anatomy Robert Knox, escaped official censure but was found guilty in the court of public opinion; his career was blighted thereafter.

The trial was a sensation. Although they were not resurrectionists, William and William's spree of murder-for-money exposed the seedy underbelly of Georgian Edinburgh, where respectable physicians paid hard cash for fresh corpses, no questions asked. The reputation of the medical profession plummeted. When a cholera epidemic took hold in 1831, many doctors found themselves accused of spreading the disease in order to obtain fresh specimens. Across Scotland, those graveyards that were not already protected sprouted, almost overnight, watch-houses, watching associations and morthouses. Although bodysnatching had long been reported in newspapers and broadsides, the trial of Burke and Hare shone a new, blood-red and bright light on the crime. It is the defining moment, the cultural fulcrum, when bodysnatching tipped from being just something-bad-that-happened to an epoch-defining event.

'Burking' speedily entered popular culture and folklore. Fake tales of narrow escapes flooded the press. Burkers were said to attack people in alleyways and on lonely moors, suffocating them with poisonous sticking plasters. Friends played burking pranks on nervous companions. Tinkers or travelling people, especially in the North-East, told fearful stories of being stalked by murderous medical students. These tales were still being repeated as recent factual events over a century after the last of the bodysnatchers had disappeared. All of these kinds of folktale can be found throughout this book. Another common urban legend told of a man who substituted himself for a stolen corpse, and then 'came alive' and spoke to the terrified bodysnatchers 'from beyond the grave'.

KILLING FOR CASH BEFORE BURKE AND HARE

Eighty years before the West Port murders, two women became the first 'killers for cash' in supplying anatomical subjects. Nurses Helen Torrence and Jean Waldie had promised a doctor the body of a sick child they had been caring for. However, either the child got better or they were unable to abstract the body from the coffin, for a substitute was required. On 3 December 1751 they fixed on nine-year-old John Dallas, son of an alcoholic mother. While Torrence distracted the woman with a dram or five, Waldie kidnapped John and smothered him with her bedclothes. The doctor only offered 2s for the body, raising the price after haggling by another 10d, with 6d to pay the porter who had carried the box. Once sober, the boy's mother raised the alarm. The body, now a hot potato and evidence of murder, was found dumped in a city street four days later, 'with evident marks of its having been in the surgeons' hands.' The actual act of murder could not be proved, as there were no witnesses, so the pair were convicted of two separate crimes: kidnapping the boy, and 'selling and delivering his body, then dead, to some surgeons and students of physic'. The implied murder brought the death penalty. Torrence tried to avoid the noose by claiming to be pregnant, but this was easily disproved. Both were hanged in the Grassmarket in February 1752.

In 1826 a destitute Irishwoman offered to sell a surgeon both her healthy two-month-old son (price £7) and her thirteen-year-old boy, 'whom he could kill or boil or do what he liked with.' After her arrest she said she had previously marketed the baby to another anatomist, but had only been offered a derisory £5.

DEFENDING THE DEAD

Grave-protection methods varied over time and between parishes, depending on the amount of money available, new developments in technology, and fashion. Typical defences included: high graveyard walls and locked gates; exceptionally deep graves; and spade-frustrating layers of heather or turf mixed in with the soil. Other, more elaborate, methods included:

Mortsafes – heavy coffin-enclosing frameworks of iron bands. Variations included large iron coffins placed over the wooden one. In both cases the expensive grave-cover was usually removed after a few weeks and re-used for the next grave.
Caged lairs – basically the mortsafe idea applied to architecture, with roofs of cast-iron bars sunk into solid stone walls around 'lairs' or burial plots. In some cases an entire cage, like an animal cage, was constructed.

A caged lair from Greyfriars Cemetery, Edinburgh. *(Geoff Holder)*

An iron coffin mortsafe and watch-house at Banchory-Devenick churchyard, Aberdeenshire. *(Geoff Holder)*

Mortstones – heavy stone blocks laid over a coffin to prevent access.

Morthouses – strongholds where coffins were stored for several weeks, until their contents were of no interest to anatomists. The coffins were then buried as normal.

Watch-houses and watchtowers – structures built to shelter watchmen, armed guards who 'watched' graveyards overnight. Nervous watchers were not always reliable with a gun, as their victims included goats, horses, rams, windows, tombstones – and sometimes each other.

This book contains all the mortsafes, iron coffins, mortstones, morthouses, caged lairs and watch-houses it has been possible to locate.

Bodysnatching was subject to the same logistical problems as, say, drug-smuggling. Carriers of illegitimate goods could be stopped at 'pinchpoints' – bridges, toll-bars, city gates and ferry ports. If discovered, they risked assault and worse from enraged mobs.

AN INTERNATIONAL CRIME NETWORK

Bodysnatching was big business. It was a *de facto* industry, with regular suppliers, communications and distribution systems, a reliance on market intelligence, and a network of informants, agents, transportation captains and other freelance contractors. From Edinburgh, tendrils spread through the Lothians, Fife, Stirling, Perth and the Borders. Glasgow's agents concentrated on the west coast. Aberdeen's influence extended as far as Inverness and the Highlands.

But even with these multiple suppliers, not enough cadavers were coming through from Scottish sources. So the industry internationalised. Bodies – often tied into compact bundles and transported in boxes marked soft goods, crystal or stationery – came by coach from London or Newcastle. False name and address labels were used, with agents redirecting the items at the depot. But the biggest source was Ireland, a desperately poor country where lifted bodies were sold in bulk at discount prices. Wilson Rae, a Dublin-based Scottish doctor known as

'The Captain', had a regular trade sending over his just-expired terminal patients, visiting Edinburgh himself once or twice a year to collect the cash from Dr Knox.

The danger, however, was that the sea voyage could be delayed by weather or customs, causing the perishable 'goods' to spoil. For this reason the preferred route was usually Dublin to Liverpool, with the valued products (marked as cured pork, dry-salted beef, stuffed animals, blacking or apples) then transshipped to Scotland by stagecoach or smack. Sometimes plans went awry, as when Liverpool dockers noticed the stench from three casks marked 'Bitter salts'. Eleven bodies were found pickled in brine and packed in salt, and investigations turned up a further twenty-two in a cellar run by a gang operating out of the city. Coroners at the stagecoach-changing posts of Lancaster and Carlisle became wearily experienced at writing death certificates that simply stated, 'Found in a box in a putrefied condition.' And in February 1829 a mix-up saw Dr Knox's cadaver-handling assistant take delivery of a ham, a cheese, eggs and a roll of Hodden-grey cloth.

BODYSNATCHING AND THE LAW

Graverobbing may have outraged moral and cultural standards, but in legal terms it was a mess. Most laws of the time protected property, and technically a body was not property, so neither the corpse nor the relatives had any rights. So if a body was stolen, what crime had been committed? Most experienced bodysnatchers made sure to leave the shroud and any death-clothes behind, as to take them was evident theft. After about 1805 many judges settled on 'violating a sepulchre', the breaking open of the coffin being deemed similar to illegal entry of premises, but the sentence a convicted resurrectionist faced often depended on their own social status and the attitude and legal knowledge of the judge. Generally, but not universally, medical students were treated more leniently than lower-class criminals. By 1820, fines and sentences of imprisonment were becoming heavier.

THE DEATH OF THE RESURRECTIONISTS

Reform of the law was already in the air before Burke and Hare erupted into mass public consciousness. Eventually, dogged by compromise and impelled by a later bodysnatching scandal in London, Parliament passed the Anatomy Act of 1832. People who died in the workhouse and whose bodies were unclaimed by friends or family would now as a matter of course end up on the dissecting table. Anatomy schools were to be regulated and inspected. All cadavers coming in were to be recorded by name, and after use buried in coffins at the school's expense. It wasn't perfect, and the poor took the brunt, but it was an improvement, and bodysnatching ceased to be either a necessity or a source of profit.

In the years following 1832, several now-prominent physicians – such as Robert Liston and Sir Robert Christison – came forward with candid memoirs about their bodysnatching days.

MONEY MAKES THE WORLD GO ROUND

Money was at the heart of the bodysnatching enterprise. In a particularly brutal example of capitalism taken to its ultimate conclusion, people were literally worth more dead than alive. Corpses were offered for sale, evaluated for worth, haggled over, and then exchanged for cash. It was a market-led activity where the hard-to-obtain high-value 'product' was, despite difficult trading conditions, continuously supplied by independent contractors due to increased consumer demand. Prices varied as the market ebbed and flowed, with lower sums offered in summer when there were few medical students around and the bodies could not be preserved in the higher temperatures. Prices were lowest in Aberdeen and highest in Edinburgh, where a corpse in good condition in winter fetched on average £10. To put that in perspective, a stagecoach driver made £1 a week, and when Burke and Hare were working as labourers on the Forth and Clyde Canal, they earned 2s a day, a sum similar to that earned by agricultural workers. So a decent corpse paid the equivalent of three months' hard labour. No wonder there were people willing to do the dirty work.

The 1820s of course used the pre-decimal money system of £ s d, where twelve pennies (12d) made one shilling (1s) and 20s made £1. Other coins used included a guinea (£1 1s) and a sovereign (£1 2s).

With the exception of graveyards within walking (and corpse-carrying) distance, there were always transport expenses. In Edinburgh a porter would carry a box for 6d. Further afield, a vehicle was required. There are several cases where a carriage used for bodysnatching was destroyed by a mob. This would have represented a loss of perhaps £40-50 to the owner, less if it was a small cart, more if it was a fancier model. Horses might cost around £10 more or less, depending on the quality. Most horse-driven carriages were hired, not owned (unless the owner was pretty well-to-do). The daily rate varied, but think of it in terms of prices for hiring a car today.

WHY A GAZETTEER?

The bodysnatchers were predominantly active from the 1730s to 1832. If you come across a mortsafe or watch-house in a graveyard, you are touching a piece of a unique – and deeply strange – period in British history. But over the past few decades much of this physical heritage has vanished. Vandalism, decay and redevelopment have all taken their toll. So please use this book to explore, enjoy and marvel, before some of the physical remains go the way of all flesh.

THE GAZETTEER

The Gazetteer lists every site in Scotland where physical remains of the anti-bodysnatching days have been identified, as well as any associated stories. Each entry has the same basic structure:

THE NAME OF THE SITE (in alphabetical order within a chapter)
A summary, helping you decide if it's a site worth visiting.
Address: Including the postcode, and directions where necessary.
NGR: The National Grid Reference number, as used on Ordnance Survey maps.
Lat, Long: The Latitude (N) and Longitude (W). Between the postcode, NGR, and these grid co-ordinates, you should be able to locate a site by map, GPS, or online.
Access: Details of parking and entry, including disabled access if any. Many older graveyards, by their nature, are not wheelchair-friendly.
Things to see: The physical remains (watch-houses, mortsafes, etc.), listed and described.
Comments: Other items of interest, such as gravestones carved with eighteenth-century symbols of mortality and immortality, Pictish monuments, and other nearby historic sites.
Stories: Anecdotes, tales and documented events relating to the site. All are taken from written sources, but some stories may have become exaggerated over time.

Over 260 sites are described here. Many more used to have watch-houses or mortsafes, but in the absence of any physical remains, or a good story, they have been omitted for reasons of space.

EDINBURGH AND THE LOTHIANS

'How long will a man lie i' the earth ere he rot?'
William Shakespeare, *Hamlet*

EDINBURGH

Edinburgh provided the finest training for surgeons in the English-speaking world, attracting students from all over the British Isles and the Colonies. The various anatomy lecturers (Alexander Monro at the university, and Robert Knox, Robert Liston, the Aitken brothers, John Lizars and others within the competing private schools) were engaged in a professional war with each other, fighting tooth and nail over reputation, status, students, fees – and the availability of cadavers. It was bodysnatching central.

The Cheilead, or University Coterie, a short-lived student magazine of 1826-27, had this to say when a £10 reward was offered for the identity of those who had stolen a fisherman's body in Newhaven: 'These men perform miracles, for they "raise the dead", they are slave dealers, for they sell men; they are amusing, for they furnish subjects for conversation; scientific, for they assist science. They are a species *sui generis*; Lycanthropes, for they live on the dead; discoverers, for they bring things hidden to light; quarrelsome, for they pick holes. Of what consequence is it to the fisherman whether the shark, the worm, or the scalpel decomposed his body?' Charming.

Sometimes the corpses were taken straight out of coffins, replaced by an equal weight of waste material. In 1829 a baker starting his shift spotted a large bundle being lowered from an attic tenement while three men in the street below were actively ignoring it. After a hue and cry the package was opened, revealing a recently-deceased drummer called Nosy. Other times cadavers were stashed in quiet locations, for recovery later. In 1827 two men arrived by gig at an address in Queen Street suspiciously early. A search uncovered a young man's body hidden in the cellar.

Sometimes, of course, the street vigilantes got things wrong. One night in 1823 a coach was seen carrying a coffin from a doctor's house in the New Town. In Nicholson Street the mob released the horses, dragged the coach over The Mound, and burned it. It turned out the coach was heading for the physician's country house, where he had recently passed away. Three youths from the mob were arrested.

BUCCLEUCH CHURCHYARD
Anecdote only.
Address: 33 Chapel Street, Edinburgh, EH8 9AT.
NGR: NT26051 72950.
Lat, Long: 55.943881, -3.185549.
Access: The few gravestones around the closed church are generally accessible.
Stories: In 1818 Miss Wilson, a young beauty of Bruntsfield Links, chose Henry Ferguson as her beau in preference to George Duncan. The two suitors lodged together in Potterrow next to Buccleuch. When Ferguson died of disease, the passion-inflamed Duncan hired a professional bodysnatcher named 'the Screw' to steal the body and sell it to the anatomists. For the rest of his student days he would gloatingly spy on the young woman as she wept over a grave that was, unknown to her, empty.

A typical caged lair, in Canongate kirkyard. *(Geoff Holder)*

CANONGATE

A splendid site with numerous caged lairs and a shot-pocked stone.

Address: Canongate Kirk, 153 Canongate, Edinburgh, EH8 8DP.

NGR: NT26443 73883.

Lat, Long: 55.952314, -3.179526.

Access: The graveyard is open during daylight hours. Level access off Canongate but the site slopes severely after that, with some steps on the tarmac paths.

Things to see: 1. By and large the anti-bodysnatching fashion for Edinburgh people with money was for a stone-built vault with a gated entrance or stout door, and a metal 'cage' on the roof. Often these vaults were built in rows, taking advantage of a common rear wall. Canongate is a typical example: there are around twenty-two of such vaults, three of which still have their ironwork roof. 2. A tombstone just left of the western path bears the carving of a coach and four horses crossing a stream by an old-fashioned bridge, and the inscription 'For the Society of Coach Drivers in Canongate'. The stone is peppered with small holes, said to have been from small-shot and swan-shot fired by a watchman.

Comments: An excellent historic church in the Old Town, with many stones of interest, and the grave of economist Adam Smith, one of the key figures of the Scottish Enlightenment.

Stories: In 1811 a man called Wight from the Canongate area stole into the house where a neighbour's body lay awaiting burial, removed the corpse, and filled the coffin with sand.

COLINTON

An iron coffin and a watch-house.

Address: Colinton Church, Spylaw Street, Colinton, Edinburgh, EH13 0JP.

NGR: NT21569 69125.

Lat, Long: 55.908803, -3.256171.

Access: Level tarmac paths.

Things to see: 1. The splendid iron coffin cover is impossible to miss beside the path. This is the only survivor of six once owned by the parish. 2. The offertory house adjacent to the entrance was also used as a watch-house.

Comments: Parish minister Lewis Balfour was Robert Louis Stevenson's grandfather, and the young RLS played in the graveyard.

CRAMOND

A watch-house and morthouse in a lovely setting.

Address: Cramond Kirk, Cramond Glebe Road, Cramond, Edinburgh, EH4 6NT

NGR: NT18945 76845.

Lat, Long: 55.977714, -3.300459.

Access: Small parking area opposite. Otherwise, follow car park signs to rear of graveyard. Wheelchair ramp, good paths.

Things to see: 1. The attractive watch-house just left of the gate was originally a Session

House (and is still used for that purpose today). Two or more men were stationed here, armed with an impromptu range of clubbing weapons. 2. What was very likely a morthouse stands beside the entrance to Kirk Cramond, the path north of the church. It now houses electrical equipment. 3. The three stone-built family lairs probably had iron cages for roofs, but these have vanished.

Comments: An immaculately-kept graveyard, with a church on a site that has been Christian since the sixth century. The outline of the predecessor Roman fort is laid out, and there are many excellent gravestones from the seventeenth and eighteenth centuries.

CURRIE

A mortstone.

Address: Currie Parish Church, 17 Kirkgate, Currie, EH14 6AN.
NGR: NT18301 67655.
Lat, Long: 55.89287, -3.301459.
Access: Many steps.
Things to see: A bemossed mortstone lies in the grass.
Comments: A very fine kirk.

DRUMMOND STREET/SURGEONS' SQUARE

The vastly-changed site of what was once bodysnatching central.

Address: University of Edinburgh, Drummond Street, Edinburgh, EH8 9TT.
NGR: NT261733.
Lat, Long: 55.947539, -3.184540.
Access: City street and university urban campus.
Things to see: No trace of the Royal Infirmary remains, but the ornamental gates form the entrance to the Geography building. Surgeons' Square is further east, behind the Department of Archaeology. Dr Knox' s house and most of the other anatomists' buildings have gone, but Chisholm House (now the Institute of Governance and the Science Studies Unit) remains as a typical example of the surgeons' mansions that once lined the Square.
Stories: The Infirmary had its own small cemetery for the burial of those who died alone in hospital. As can be imagined, this was highly convenient for the medical students, but convenience created friction. A full-scale fight broke out between rival groups over the body of crippled ballad singer Sandie McNab, with the noise attracting the watch; in the confusion one student used ropes and pulleys to haul the boxed body up to an anatomist's upper-storey window. On another occasion two adventurer-anatomists, Mowbray Thomson and Robert Liston, confronted each other over a grave. Although outnumbered (and Liston also had the violent ex-boxer Ben Crouch with him), Thomson stood his ground, flourishing a dagger and then a pistol. Things could have turned nasty but Thomson's reinforcements arrived, so Liston's gang opted for a tactical retreat. On another occasion, at an unnamed graveyard Liston's party was disturbed by the watch; under gunfire he escaped, running with an adult corpse under each arm.

In 1826 a porter trundling a large box into the square was set upon by a mob intent on killing him. When rescued by the police he explained his cargo was a llama which had died in Wombell's Menagerie, and was destined for the anatomy museum.

In 1983, workmen restoring the old town wall (still visible) found fifty-five human bones where the north-east of Surgeons' Square once stood. The assemblage represented at least five individuals, one a child of around six to eight years. Almost certainly this was an anatomist's midden.

If a broadside published at the time can be believed, John Macintire was buried alive on 15 April 1824, and brought back to screaming life in an anatomy room: 'The Demonstrator took his knife, and pierced my bosom. I felt a dreadful crackling, as it were, throughout my whole frame; a convulsive shudder instantly followed, and a shriek of horror rose from all present.' According to Macintire's testimony, he had been fully conscious from the moment he was pronounced dead, through to his burial and resurrection.

Surgeons' Square in 1829. Dr Knox's Rooms are in the centre, flanked by Surgeons' Hall (left) and Royal Medical Society (right). *(Author's Collection)*

DUDDINGSTON

An excellent watchtower and several caged lairs.
Address: Duddingston Kirk, Old Church Lane, Duddingston, EH15 3PX.
NGR: NT28349 72619.
Lat, Long: 55.941256, -3.148677.
Access: Car park beside the loch. The gate is sometimes locked. Gravel and cobbled paths.
Things to see: 1. The superb two-storey hexagonal watchtower of 1824 dominates the entrance, with its battlemented parapet and arched windows. The ground floor is used as a vestry and Session House. 2. A line of stone-built lairs includes two still with caged roofs.
Comments: The church is an utter delight, with Norman architecture, jougs, a loupin'-on stone (for mounting a horse in a genteel manner) and other treasures.
Stories: Dr Martin Eccles and professional resurrectionist John Samuel disinterred the corpse of a Miss Stewart. They had nearly finished shovelling the earth back into the grave, when the corpse gave a great sneeze. Faced with a revived young woman, the pair promptly decamped, and invented a story that the 'resurrection' was caused by the sexton attempting to steal her jewellery.

EAST PRESTON STREET

Another high quality watchtower.
Address: East Preston Street Graveyard, Edinburgh, EH8 9QF.
NGR: NT26635 72395.
Lat, Long: 55.938977, -3.176047.
Access: Street parking. A grassy, level site.
Things to see: The impressive two-storey castellated watchtower overlooks the whole site. Dated 1820 and in good condition, it has an external staircase and a ground-floor door.
Comments: A wee gem in the city.

GILMERTON

Anecdote only.
Three inexperienced medical students lifted a woman from a graveyard somewhere near here, but forgot to bring a sack for the body. One man therefore hoisted it on his back, secured by the shroud. As he staggered along, the corpse's feet bounced off the ground, giving the illusion of movement. Crying 'She's alive!' the tyro dumped his burden and scarpered along with his equally-spooked colleagues. The following morning the widower found his wife's body by the roadside, and, until the situation was explained to him, thought to his horror that she had been buried alive.

GREYFRIARS

A massive and justly-celebrated site. Essential.
Address: Greyfriars Kirk, Forrest Road/ Candlemaker Row, Edinburgh, EH1 2QQ.
NGR: NT25634 73264.
Lat, Long: 55.946629, -3.192312.
Access: Entrance up a slightly inclined cobbled lane called Greyfriars. Paved, tarmac and gravel paths on a site that slopes in all directions, with some steps in the further regions. Wheelchair users with assistance should be able to see most of the sights. A visitor centre in the church itself is open from Easter to October, 10.30 a.m. to 4.30 p.m. Monday to Friday, and 10.30 a.m. to 2.30 p.m. on Saturday.

The caged lair of surgeon William Inglis, Greyfriars Cemetery. Presumably he knew the importance of defending the dead. *(Geoff Holder)*

Things to see: 1. A double mortsafe consisting of a low framework of bars on all four sides, the upper cage displaying two inscribed stone slabs, dated 1829. An adjacent stone-lined rectangle retains one remaining bar of its former metal cover. 2. James Borthwick's tombstone on the eastern gable of the church. Borthwick was the first anatomist mentioned in the Edinburgh records, taking up his post in 1645 as a 'Master Surgeon' with specific responsibility for giving instruction in anatomy. This was at the time when the Incorporation of Surgeons were still a subset of the Guild of Barbers. As well as a dancing skeleton, his memorial is notable for its depiction of knives, scalpels, syringes and other items from the seventeenth-century anatomist's kit-bag. 3. The three-windowed watch-house with its tall chimney. Standing at the entrance, it is now used as a base for ghost tours, and rejoices in the rubric of 'The Creepy Wee Shop in the Graveyard'. 4. There are a dozen stone-built family lairs in the main graveyard, of which four still retain their caged roofs. Several are decorated with skulls, bones and other symbols. There are probably another ten or so similar lairs in the 'Covenanters' Aisle', a section which is usually kept locked; hundreds of those who had signed the National Covenant to protest against the religious policies or Charles I were imprisoned here in 1679, in the open air without shelter – many perished. 5. One of the lairs has a different structure, being a solid, entirely closed-in building with a pitched roof, stout door and a ventilation hole. Although described as a family vault, its nature suggests it may have functioned as a morthouse. 6. The domed neo-Classical monument of Sir George Mackenzie is locked, but looking through the door you can catch sight of a metal anti-snatcher grille set into the floor of the subterranean crypt. This imposing structure is supposedly haunted by the 'Mackenzie Poltergeist'.

A 'double bedder' mortsafe at Greyfriars. *(Geoff Holder)*

Comments: The quintessential spooky Scottish urban graveyard, with numerous elaborate monuments, countless representa-

The watch-house at Greyfriars, now 'The Creepy Wee Shop in the Graveyard'. *(Geoff Holder)*

tions of mortality, the grave of the faithful dog Greyfriars Bobby, and endless tour groups.

Stories: Greyfriars is the site of the first recorded act of bodysnatching in Scotland, in 1678. On 6 February of that year four gypsies of the name of Shaw were hanged for murdering a man of the Faws family, in what was described as a clan battle between various gypsy cadres from both Scotland and Ireland. The following morning the mass grave at Greyfriars was found to be disturbed, the body of the sixteen-year-old youngest malefactor being missing. Some thought he had not died on the scaffold and had revived in the grave, but most believed, along with a contemporary commentator, that, 'His body was stolen away by some chirurgeon, or his servant, to make ane anatomicale dissection on.'

In another very early case, the corpse of Robert Findlay was stolen from the graveyard in 1711. A long satirical poem of limited quality, published in a broadside, placed the blame on both the gravediggers and the surgeons:

These monsters of mankind, who made the graves,
To the chirurgeons became hired slaves;
They rais'd the dead again out of the dust,
And sold to them, to satisfy their lust.
As I'm inform'd, the chirurgeons did give
Forty shillings for each one they receive:
And they their flesh and bones assunder part,
Which wounds their living friends unto the heart.

The Incorporation of Surgeons, for their part, denied any wrong-doing and stated they would expel any member guilty of such a terrible crime. Well, that worked.

Another Greyfriars sepulchre was violated in 1725, leading to a further broadside, this one entitled: *Groans from the grave: or, complaints of the dead, against the surgeons for raising their bodies out of the dust.* Vigorous popular protests saw the windows smashed at the Surgeons' Square home of Alexander Monro the First; Monro and his associates were in fear of their lives, and soon after moved the dissecting equipment and specimens into the university buildings for greater security.

There is a rumour that a wealthy old lady was accidentally buried alive at Greyfriars, only to be revived to consciousness when the bodysnatchers were roughly removing the costly rings from her fingers. Although such cases of premature burial were not unknown at the time, I have a suspicion that this particular case is just a good story.

LEITH

Watchmen's weapons and some fine caged lairs.

Address: South Leith Parish Church, Kirkgate pedestrian precinct, Leith, EH6 6BG.
NGR: NT27043 76066.
Lat, Long: 55.972015, -3.170519.
Access: Disabled parking and access at church. For entry, phone 0131 554 2578 (1.30 p.m. to 4.30 p.m., Monday to Friday).
Things to see: 1. The watchers were originally issued with firearms but this, combined with their standard refreshment of a barrel of beer, proved too dangerous to persons and property, so after an unfortunate

One of the two watchmen's batons in South Leith Kirk.
(*Courtesy of Kirk Session of South Leith parish church*)

drunken episode batons were substituted. Two of these batons can be seen in a display case within the west porch, along with a pair of watchmen's caps which look like they belong on a Grand National jockey. 2. One standalone and several contiguous caged lairs, still retaining their iron framework roofs.

Comments: A lovely old churchyard in an urban setting.

Stories: An astonishingly early case of bodysnatching took place in 1721. In the Kirk Record of 5 January, 'Francis Thomson reported that he and John Weir, having searched the grave where the corps of Ann Wright was buried, they found the chist [coffin] in the grave, but the corpse away.' The Session appointed a committee of Elders to investigate this and 'several other gross abuses' committed in the churchyard. There was a watch-house by 1735 but this and a later structure are long gone.

LIBERTON

A good watch-house.

Address: Liberton Parish Church, Kirkgate, Liberton, Edinburgh, EH16 6RY.

NGR: NT27512 69528.

Lat, Long: 55.913352, -3.161246.

Access: Car park at Liberton Hall. Level tarmac paths.

Things to see: The standard watch-house at the gate is in good condition.

Comments: An excellent church with an outstanding collection of carved tombstones.

Stories: In 1828 John McQuilkan was arrested near a disturbed grave, with a rope, sack and shovel nearby. His defence was that he had never seen the items before, but given the circumstances and the fact that he was a porter who lived next to the Royal Infirmary and Surgeons' Square, the court did not believe him. He was imprisoned for six months. Around the same period, Andrew Ewart mistakenly shot and killed his friend and fellow watcher Henry Pennycook. His defence council stated in court that, 'in making his rounds on a dark night, he came suddenly on a man skulking round the church; he saw that he

was armed,' and that he acted 'in the discharge, as he thought, of a sacred and imperative duty'. Ewart was given the death sentence, later commuted to twelve months' imprisonment.

NATIONAL MUSEUM OF SCOTLAND

Address: Chambers Street, Edinburgh, EH1 1JF.

NGR: NT258733.

Lat, Long: 55.946991, -3.189183.

Access: Open 10 a.m. to 5 p.m. daily, admission free. Wheelchair access throughout.

Things to see: The display Daith Comes In (...an it's no particular who it takes awa') within the Industry and Empire section has a mortsafe from Airth, Falkirk, and a corpse collar from Kingskettle, Fife. The latter was bolted through the bottom of the coffin and round the neck of the body.

Comments: You could spend weeks here.

NEW CALTON CEMETERY

A spectacular watchtower and several caged lairs.

Address: Regent Road, Edinburgh, EH8 8DR.

NGR: NT26645 74014.

Lat, Long: 55.953519, -3.17632.

Access: The site is virtually invisible from Regent Road. Look for the unsignposted tarmac path east of the prominent domed Burns Monument. It slopes steeply downhill as the graveyard descends in a series of terraces, with steps. A challenging site for anyone with disabilities.

Things to see: 1. The massive three-storey watchtower broods from high over the cascading cemetery. Built in 1820, the battlemented parapet and curved external staircase add to the sense of defence and protection. Badly fire-damaged and home to heroic quantities of pigeon guano, it is still an impressive structure. 2. Adjacent to the tower is a stone lair that still retains its caged roof. At least another forty-odd similar lairs adorn the cemetery; most are roofless, but four are still in possession of the roof-cage. 3. The boundary walls are noticeably high.

Comments: Panoramic views over the Scottish Parliament and Arthur's Seat.

The watchtower at New Calton Cemetery, seen through the now-roofless arch of a caged lair. *(Geoff Holder)*

A pentagonal iron roof frame in a caged lair at New Calton. *(Geoff Holder)*

A fully-enclosed iron caged lair at Old Calton Cemetery. *(Geoff Holder)*

OLD CALTON CEMETERY

Address: Waterloo Place, Edinburgh, EH1 3BQ.

NGR: NT26029 74020.

Lat, Long: 55.953483, -3.186191.

Access: The entrance pierces the grim stolid façade by a bus stop on the south side of the street. This is not a site for anyone with mobility difficulties, as there are many steps and steep inclines. The site is cut in two by Waterloo Place, with a handbag-sized section on the north side. To reach it, take the road marked Calton Hill and turn left up the steps by the Parliament House Hotel.

Things to see: 1. Of the thirty or so individual family vaults, four still have their cages of iron protecting the roof. There is one, roofless, lair, in the 'orphaned' northern section. 2. A lair protected by an elaborate iron cage. 3. The dominating circular mausoleum of David Hume (1711-76), rationalist philosopher and key figure in the Scottish Enlightenment. Hume suspected his body might be of interest to the anatomists, so before his death he set aside a sum of money to ensure a watch would be posted on his grave. The ornate domed structure was erected a year after he was buried. 4. Note again the very high anti-snatcher walls.

Comments: A very rewarding site, even more Gothic than New Calton, with highly decorated stones, an enormous obelisk in memory of eighteenth-century political martyrs, and a memorial (complete with statues of Abraham Lincoln and a freed slave) to the Scottish soldiers who fought in the American Civil War. Note that several of the vaults are the sleeping quarters of homeless people.

PORTOBELLO

A mortsafe.

Address: Old Parish Church, Bellfield Street, Portobello, EH15 2BP.

NGR: NT30880 73809.

Lat, Long: 55.952317, -3.108471.

Access: Level access.

Things to see: A mortsafe resides in the graveyard.

Comments: A fine church.

RESTALRIG

One man's attempt to not be snatched.

Address: Old Parish Church, Restalrig Road South, Edinburgh, EH7 6LF.
NGR: NT28337 74483.
Lat, Long: 55.957999, -3.149365.
Access: Tarmac paths.
Things to see: The closed tomb with the Classical pediment by the west door of the church houses the mortal remains of Louis Cauvin (died 1825), a wealthy teacher of French with an abiding fear of the resurrectionists. His Will stated, 'My corpse is to be deposited in Restalrig churchyard and watched for a proper time. The door of the tomb must be taken off, and the space built up strongly with ashlar stones. The tomb must be shut for ever, and never to be opened.'
Comments: St Triduana's Well in the graveyard is cared for by Historic Scotland (call 0131 554 7400 in advance to gain entry).

ST CUTHBERT'S

Another excellent watchtower.

Address: Lothian Road, Edinburgh, EH1 2EP.
NGR: NT24760 73546.
Lat, Long: 55.949482, -3.205567.
Access: Steps down from the street. Tarmac paths.
Things to see: The restored cylindrical watchtower of 1827 is an obvious sight at the junction with Kings Stables Road. The second storey has a crenellated parapet and multiple windows overlooking the extensive graveyard. Note also the graveyard walls – raised to 8ft (2.5m) in 1738 after an early bodysnatching incident – and several lairs which used to have metal gates.
Comments: The atmospheric site used to be called the West Kirkyard.
Stories: A corpse stolen in 1742 sparked a season of riot and destruction. On 9 March the body of Alexander Baxter was found in an empty house adjoining the premises of surgeon Martin Eccles. At a period when the authorities literally 'drummed up' attention, the city guard's drum was stolen and beat along the Cowgate, calling the mob to arms. Eccles' shop was demolished, other surgeons' houses were attacked, and the riot was quelled with difficulty. Probably to restore public order more than anything else, Eccles and his students were arrested, but the charges were dropped for want of proof. The mob, thus frustrated, then acted on a rumour that George Haldane, one of the West Kirk beadles, was a snatcher. In a riot lasting through the night and morning of 15-16 March, Haldane's house was burnt to the ground. The place was dubbed 'resurrection hall', this being the first use of the term resurrection or resurrectionist in connection with graverobbing. Both Haldane and another beadle were removed from office by the church, so perhaps the rumours were true. The month saw another couple of incidents, ending on the 26th with the seizure of a street-chair containing a body. This time the authorities took control of the situation, with the chairmaster and carrier banished from the city and the chair itself burned by the public executioner. This seemed to defuse the frenzy, and things were quiet for a few years.

In 1803 a regular watch was set up. In 1825 two men fled the graveyard at 5 a.m., dumping a sack containing the body of an old woman. Two years later three snatchers escaped over the wall after being fired on, leaving behind tools and traces of blood. The following night they were foiled again. In 1839 the watch was noted as owning '1 gun, 1 blunderbuss, 2 powder flasks'. The Anatomy Act of 1832 ordered legally-dissected cadavers to be buried in a coffin, and the names of the deceased recorded. In Edinburgh, the chosen site for such depositions was St Cuthbert's.

SURGEONS' HALL MUSEUMS

An essential visit for Burke-and-Hare-philes.

Address: Royal College of Surgeons, Nicolson Street, Edinburgh EH8 9DW.
NGR: NT260732.

Lat, Long: 55.946745, -3.184900.

Access: Open weekdays, 12 p.m. to 4 p.m. Admission charge. Wheelchair access to some galleries – improvements are being made.

Things to see: 1. The death-mask of William Burke and a pocketbook inscribed EXECUTED 28 JANY 1829, made from his skin after he was publicly dissected by Professor Alexander Monro the Third. 2. A mannequin of Dr Robert Knox, with his flamboyant clothes and damaged eye, set in a surgeon's office. 3. The skeleton of a child suffering from hydrocephalus. Being an obvious target for interested surgeons, the grave on the Fife coast had been closely guarded. Robert Liston and Ben Crouch (with Crouch playing the part of a gentleman and a gentleman's servant) bested the competing resurrectionists by lifting the body in daylight and driving away in a carriage minutes before the watchmen came on duty.

Comments: The histories of surgery, pathology and dentistry are all covered here. A fabulously gruesome educational experience.

UNIVERSITY OF EDINBURGH, ANATOMY RESOURCE CENTRE

The bones of Mr Burke.

Address: College of Medicine and Veterinary Medicine, University Medical School, Teviot Place, Edinburgh, EH8 9AG.

NGR: NT257730.

Lat, Long: 55.944410, -3.190305.

Access: The collection (they've dropped the word 'museum') of human and animal specimens is only open to medical or veterinary students. It is, however, usually visitable on Doors Open Day in September. No wheelchair access.

Things to see: After his execution William Burke was publicly dissected, with thousands turning up to file past the corpse before the scalpel went in. His articulated skeleton now hangs in a display case, next to that of 'Howison, The Cramond Murderer', the last felon dissected before the Anatomy Act of 1832 removed that penalty for murder. Burke was dissected by Alexander Monro, the third

man of that name and family to hold the post of Professor of Anatomy. Before disposing of the remains, Monro kept the skin (later made into leather souvenirs) and some hair from a leg, then with his quill, wrote: 'This is written with the blood of Wm Burke, who was hanged at Edinburgh on 28th Jan. 1829 for the Murder of Mrs Campbell or Docherty. The blood was taken from his head on the 1st of Fe. 1829.'

Comments: Take advantage of any open days – and go!

WEST PORT

Address: 'Edinburgh's Famous Burke & Hare' Pub, 2 High Riggs, West Port, EH3 9BX

NGR: NT250731.

Lat, Long: 55.945642, -3.202256.

Access: Entry £5.

Comments: This is a strip bar. It is not clear if the 'fame' in the title refers to Messrs Burke and Hare, or the 'entertainment' within.

🙂 🙂 🙂 🙂 🙂 🙂 🙂 🙂 🙂 🙂 🙂 🙂 🙂 🙂 🙂 🙂

EAST LOTHIAN

Surgeon Robert Christison recalled one of his bodysnatching episodes at an unnamed country churchyard. When the party arrived they found a light burning in the vestry window. Somewhat fearfully, a scout crawled over the wall when suddenly the vestry door opened and a man stepped out and fired a musket. It appeared they had been discovered, but then the watcher casually sauntered back inside, only to repeat the random firing thirty minutes later. The lazy watchman never actually patrolled the graveyard, so the snatchers entered, disinterred their chosen corpse, paused while another random shot was fired and then left unmolested with their prize.

BOLTON

A splendid mortsafe.

Address: Parish Church, Bolton, EH41 4HL (on the B6368 south of Haddington).

NGR: NT50730 70073.

Lat, Long: 55.921203, -2.789949.

Access: Parking in the village. Level access to a slightly sloping grassy site with gravel paths. The church is usually open – if not, ask around for the key.

Things to see: Hanging in the porch is a splendid mortsafe, consisting of a coffin-shaped flat grid that was held in place by 28 long iron rods (two of which are on display) screwed into the ground using an elaborate series of bespoke nuts and spanners. This ensured that the 'graveguard' could not be lifted using standard tools.

Comments: Good symbolic stones and a fine mausoleum complete the visit.

Stories: In 1820 Gilbert Burns, Robert Burns' brother, wrote that their mother, Agnes Broun, had recently passed away at Bolton. Gilbert stated that the funeral would be delayed while he had a mortsafe made to defend the grave. It is not clear if this is the graveguard on display.

DIRLETON

A good watch-house.

Address: Parish Church, Manse Road, Dirleton, EH39 5HF.

NGR: NT51267 84183.

Lat, Long: 56.048009, -2.783924.

Access: Parking nearby. The church is off the village green, with level access and gravel paths.

Things to see: The large building at the gates was probably a Session House that was pressed into service for watching.

Comments: Dirleton Castle is nearby.

DUNBAR

A caged lair and a watch-house.

Address: Parish Church, Queens Road, Dunbar, EH42 1JX.

NGR: NT68176 78582.

Lat, Long: 55.999113, -2.511825.

Access: Parking in the town. Packed earth paths.

Things to see: 1. An overgrown rectangular stone lair still has the complete metal framework roof and ironwork gate.

There are several memorials within. 2. The red sandstone watch-house is roofless and doorless, allowing you to inspect the blocked-up Gothic windows, fireplace and the hint of a porch.

Comments: A grassy, exposed site dominated by the landmark church.

DUNS

Anecdote only.

One night two farmers in Duns for market day got steadfastly blootered at the White Swan. Eventually they wove their unsteady way home on the Longformacus road. Around Langton they heard a carriage coming up behind them and resolved to blag a lift, by persuasion if necessary. One man caught the horse, and the other sprang up into the gig, prepared to argue with the travellers – but two of the three passengers promptly jumped off and legged it to a nearby wood. Puzzled, the drunken farmer addressed the remaining man, only to discover it was a corpse in a suit of clothes and hat. The midnight scene now resolved into a pair of intoxicated but rapidly-sobering men, a dead body, and an abandoned horse and trap. All parties promptly returned to the hotel in Duns, where they knocked up the proprietor, Mr Jamieson, who stabled the horse and arranged for the care of the body. The following day the locals broke into the coach-house and burned the gig in the market place, and would have killed the horse as well if the beast had not been guarded. About three weeks later Mr Jamieson received a letter from a horse-hirer in Edinburgh, who wanted his property back. He was advised to collect the horse late at night, so as to avoid being assaulted.

EAST LINTON

A good watch-house and a better story.

Address: Prestonkirk Church, Preston Road, Preston, East Linton, EH40 3DS.

NGR: NT59219 77849.

Lat, Long: 55.991514, -2.654834.

Access: Car park at the church hall. A couple of low steps at the gate. Paved paths.

Things to see: A fine watch-house with arched windows.

Comments: Several good stones.

Stories: There's nothing like a bit of double-crossing between bodysnatchers. On 5 January 1819 Catherine Mack was buried at Prestonkirk. The next day Mr Gibb, the Linton postmaster, received an anonymous letter stating that an attempt would be made to lift the body. The writer claimed the warning was 'a point of honour' and signed himself 'Justice'. That night Gibb, the local policeman Ralph Plain and two strong village lads lay in wait, all armed with muskets and cudgels, while Plain also had his police-issue pistol. Three men came over the wall, one acting as the lookout while the others dug into the grave by the light of a shaded lantern. The watching party advanced and Plain fired his pistol, after which the trio surrendered. Firstly they were made to fill in the grave – at gunpoint – and then they were marched through the night to the tollbooth at Haddington. There must have been a horse-driven cart somewhere nearby but the triumphant watchers did not search for it and so it vanished, along with the driver. The Prestonkirk gravedigger later remembered two strangers asking questions about the dead woman as they watched him dig the grave.

The trial at the High Court in Edinburgh revealed the usual shenanigans. Firstly, it was postponed from March to July, probably to wait for the university to close for the summer, thus avoiding any unpleasant mob-based repercussions for the fine gentlemen of the medical profession. This was a good ruse, as the trio of miscreants turned out to include George Campbell, the servant of Edinburgh surgeon Robert Allan, and George Mclaren, the servant of Dr John Smith, physician of Edinburgh (the third man, John Weir, was a labourer with no direct link to the anatomists). All expressed great remorse, saying they were poor men tempted by the money, and this was the first time they had ever done this, honest guv. They were each sentenced to twelve months' impris-

onment. The most interesting revelation came when they recognised the handwriting on the anonymous letter. It belonged to a man who called himself Lawrie, someone they trusted. It sounds like 'Lawrie' belonged to a rival gang, and double-crossed the trio to get them out of the way. Or could he have been Dr Lawrie, imprisoned for bodysnatching a few miles away at Coldingham in Berwickshire (The Borders) just a year later?

GULLANE
A broken mortstone.

Address: St Andrew's Old Parish Church, Main Street, Gullane, EH31 2AG.

NGR: NT48032 82719.

Lat, Long: 56.034521, -2.835562.

Access: A grassy, slightly uneven site.

Things to see: A few yards from the southern wall of the ruined medieval kirk are two halves of a broken mortstone, one of which has two iron rings used for connecting to the lifting tackle.

Comments: A nice, quiet site.

MUSSELBURGH
Anecdotes only.

Address: St Michael's Parish Church, Inveresk Village Road, Inveresk, Musselburgh EH21 7UA.

NGR: NT34432 72069.

Lat, Long: 55.937185, -3.051176.

Access: Tarmac paths.

Comments: A historically-interesting kirkyard.

Stories: On 18 March 1742, following the riot related to St Cuthbert's in Edinburgh a week earlier, the house of Inveresk gardener and snatching-suspect Peter Richardson was burned to the ground. Richardson was believed to supply a confederate named Cochran with bodies from Inveresk; Musselburgh and Fisherow had also been part of Cochran's transport operation.

Inveresk continued to be a target into the nineteenth century. On one occasion a party of bodysnatchers were scared off by the watchers, leaving behind their getaway vehicle.

The enraged mob smashed and burned the gig at the market cross. Unfortunately it proved to be a carriage for hire, and the town had to foot the bill when the legitimate owner claimed damages for the destruction of his property. On a later occasion a pair of medical students were collared in the act of lifting a cadaver. They were temporarily held in a private house but asked to be locked up in jail for their own safety – and none too soon, as the jail was swiftly surrounded by a crowd armed with axes and other impromptu weapons. The duo made bail, and it is not clear if they were ever prosecuted.

OLDHAMSTOCKS

A fine watch-house.
Address: Oldhamstocks Parish Church, on a minor road west from Oldhamstocks, TD13 5XN (near Cocksburnpath).
NGR: NT73797 70626.
Lat, Long: 55.928217, -2.420898.
Access: Grassy and a little uneven, with some gravel paths.
Things to see: The watch-house of 1824 is in good nick, with an arched window and chimney. The dedication plaque above the door is now barely legible but used to read: 'And the whole valley of the dead bodies and of the ashes shall be holy unto the Lord: it shall not be plucked up or thrown down any more' (Jeremiah 31 v 40).
Comments: An attractive white-harled church in a country setting.

ORMISTON

Anecdotes only.
Address: Parish Church, Main Street, Ormiston, EH35 5HT.
NGR: NT41439 69319.
Lat, Long: 55.913414, -2.938392.
Access: Level access from pavement through gates.
Comments: The present church only dates from 1936.
Stories: A case from 1816 clearly demonstrated the way that suspected bodysnatchers were treated by the legal system if they were 'people of quality'. On 7 January the grave of William Todd, a mason in his sixties, was found empty five days after his funeral. An initial investigation by the Sheriff Officers came up with no leads, but they pointedly did not question the prime suspects, the Wright family of Westerbyres Farm. Alexander, the eldest son, had served as a surgeon with the Edinburgh Militia. His brothers David and Andrew were a doctor and medical student respectively. However, the head of the family was a wealthy farmer who employed most people in Ormiston and dominated the local economy. No one wanted to ruffle those feathers. The body was never recovered and the case was quietly dropped.

Some months later James Todd, minister of Mauchline in Ayrshire and William's brother, attended the General Assembly of the Church of Scotland in Edinburgh. There he discovered that, in his letters about his brother's case, the Ormiston minister had been economical with the *verité*. Specifically, the minister had omitted to mention that the Wrights were behind it. The energetic James Todd swung into action, undertook a proper investigation, and then gave the names of witnesses to the Sheriff. Two of the Wrights' former servants, parlourmaid Jean Grierson and kitchenmaid Jean McDonald, told how on the night of 2 January David and Andrew Wright had been out most of the evening, taking the lantern with them. The next morning the teenage girls found the outhouse locked, which meant they could not churn the butter. They gained access through a broken window – and then stumbled over a body wrapped in an old blanket. The terrified duo fled. That morning there was no breakfast awaiting the Wrights. Mrs Wright flew into a fury, but on hearing the reason why, everything changed. Suddenly there was a great deal of activity, the outhouse window was boarded up, a mysterious large barrel appeared where the body had once lain, and the houseboy was despatched to Edinburgh with an urgent letter for Dr Aitken. The Aitken brothers arrived by gig that evening and after dinner loaded the barrel on the gig.

The three Wright brothers were questioned. Alexander said he had been in Ireland with the militia on the date in question, but regimental records proved him wrong. By the time a warrant was issued he had conveniently taken up a post on a research ship in the South Atlantic, and would be away for five years. Both Andrew and David declined to answer questions. With no body as evidence, and the only witnesses being a pair of teenage servants, the case was dropped.

In contrast to the cool machinations of the Wrights, a case from 1825 seems like rank amateurism. Three graves appeared to have been opened at random, with predictably poor results. One was a child who had been in the ground for several months, another an old man in a similar state of putrefaction, and the third an elderly woman, two months buried, who had been removed from her smashed coffin but was then left lying on the grave. All three bodies, plus the shrouds and coffin parts, were simply left scattered around. The distress this caused can be imagined. The parish subsequently invested in mortsafes, but none have survived.

PENCAITLAND
Two watch-houses.
Address: Pentcaitland Parish Church, Park View, Easter Pentcaitland, EH34 5DL.
NGR: NT44323 69017.
Lat, Long: 55.911013, -2.892235.
Access: Park at the Winton Arms. Flat access on gravel paths, although the graveyard itself is grassy and uneven.
Things to see: The graveyard boasts two watch-houses, each roofed with red tiles, with one distinguished by its taller chimneystack.
Comments: The many excellent gravestones and the architecturally-interesting church make for a satisfying visit.
Stories: The story goes that two snatchers were caught in the act of digging up a grave; one was tied to the market cross and suffered at the hands of the angry villagers.

PRESTONPANS
A watch-house with skull.
Address: Prestongrange Parish Church, Kirk Street, Prestonpans, EH32 9DX.
NGR: NT38819 74561.
Lat, Long: 55.960142, -2.98153.
Access: Several steps at entrance. Tarmac paths.
Things to see: The watch-house by the gates has a skull-and-crossbones above the boarded-up window, and other moulded stone below.
Comments: A fine church with many good stones.

SPOTT
A good watch-house.
Address: Parish Church, High Road, Spott, EH42 1HX (on a minor road south of Dunbar).
NGR: NT67370 75586.
Lat, Long: 55.972309, -2.524517.
Access: Four steps descend from the gate onto the gravel paths.
Things to see: The L-shaped watch-house beside the gate boasts a chimney, porch, several windows and two doors. It is now used as a vestry and Session House.
Comments: A slightly austere T-plan kirk, enlivened by several good gravestones and the old jougs hanging outside the door.

TRANENT
Anecdote only.
Address: Parish Church, Church Street, Tranent, EH33 1BW.
NGR: NT40270 73381.
Lat, Long: 55.949733, -2.958029.
Access: Parking at the church. Tarmac paths. A slight incline.
Comments: Another superb set of Lothian gravestones. Adjacent is an excellent doocot dated 1587.
Stories: According to Peter McNeill's *Tranent and its Surroundings*, published in 1883, the village was home to about a dozen bodysnatchers, 'a crew of as notorious villains as ever disgraced a community.' Chief among

them was Henry Steel, the gravedigger, who was reputed to lift bodies within thirty minutes of the funeral. Steel's activities made him wealthy, and he bought property in the area, one field of which was known derisively as 'Grave's End'.

❦❦❦❦❦❦❦❦❦❦❦❦❦❦❦❦❦

MIDLOTHIAN

CRICHTON
Anecdote only.
Address: Crichton Collegiate Church, cul-de-sac off Colegate Road, Crichton, EH37 5XA.
NGR: NT38082 61614.
Lat, Long: 55.843747, -2.990362.
Access: Signposted from Crichton. Car park on site. Paved paths. The site slopes a tad.
Comments: The church is a mighty Victorianised medieval structure. A path from the car park leads to rugged Crichton Castle, in the care of Historic Scotland. The two sites make for a splendid visit.
Stories: A young man from a respectable family was buried in a grave 13ft deep in September 1823. Two days later a cloud of black maggot flies covered the opened grave, with the coffin broken and torn linen scattered around. The chaos suggested the snatchers had been disturbed in the act.

DALKEITH
A striking watchtower and a wealth of stories.
Address: New Burial-ground, Old Edinburgh Road, Dalkeith, EH22 1JB
NGR: NT33017 67273.
Lat, Long: 55.893906, -3.072632.
Access: Gates near junction with Eskbank Road. Car park opposite. Grassed site with slight rise at entrance.
Things to see: 1. The impressive red sandstone watchtower that dominates the graveyard is a two-storeyed affair with battlements, slit windows and six sides, looking for all the world like a miniature castle. It was built in 1827 at a cost of £150. There is usually no access to its interior except on Doors Open Day in September. The tower was restored in the mid-1980s by the Dalkeith History Society. 2. Turn right at the gate then right at North Wynd. Hidden in the graveyard wall is a blocked-up entrance, the subject of a dispute between the Committee for the Protection of the New Burying Ground, and the church. The leaders of the Committee wanted the right to use this door to sneak up on the watchtower to ensure the watchers were alert and not asleep; the church disputed this exclusive access to their property, and after much argument they appear to have won.
Comments: Nineteenth-century tombstones in a site with high walls.
Stories: The Committee first tried using several mortsafes manufactured by James McGill the Dalkeith blacksmith, but these proved to be troublesome, awkward and expensive to deploy. In 1823 the Kirk Session ordered that, 'in future no person shall use cart and horse for conveying within the churchyard safes or any other thing as the grass and gravestones have of late been much injured by this practice.' The sexton was granted an additional 1s fee when a mortsafe was used. In the end the watchtower replaced the mortsafes.

A curious case took place in 1827. On 1 March William Thomson, found guilty of highway robbery, had been hanged in Dalkeith High Street. A Mr Drylee approached William King, the gravedigger, and offered him £20 (a very large sum, possibly a preposterous one) if he would lay Thomson in a shallow grave and maintain a watch in preparation for the body being lifted. The operation was thwarted by a heavy snowfall. Intriguingly, 'Drylee' had posed as a doctor but was actually a baker; he was presumably an agent for other parties in Edinburgh. Thomson was also alleged to have sold a head 'in a fresh state' to a medical student for 3s. He was summoned to the Kirk Session to face these charges, all of which he denied. The following year, Tommy Brown the bellman was also suspected of snatching, but the charge was not proved.

The restored battlemented watchtower at Dalkeith. *(Geoff Holder)*

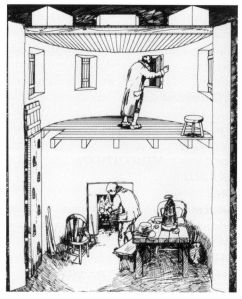

The interior arrangement within the Dalkeith watchtower. Communication between the two storeys was by ladder. *(Dalkeith History Society)*

In 1828 a book was published entitled *The Life of Mansie Wauch, Tailor in Dalkeith, Written by Himself*. It purported to be the autobiography of a humble tailor but was in fact a novel written by David Macbeth Moir, a surgeon from Musselburgh, and originally appeared in magazine form in 1824. The resurrectionists are the subject of one chapter: 'Some loons were playing false with the kirkyard, howking up the bodies from their damp graves, and harling them away to the College. Words cannot describe the fear, and the dool, and the misery it caused.' Four graves are found ransacked, including that of an infant taken with its coffin.

Mansie's turn comes up to spend a night watching the graveyard, and his fears come to the fore: 'It was a frightful thing to be out of one's bed, and to be murdered in a session-house, at the dead hour of night, by unearthly resurrection-men, or rather let me call them deevils incarnate, wrapt up in dreadnoughts, with blacked faces, pistols, big sticks, and other deadly weapons.' Mansie and two colleagues drink and tell ghost stories around the fire. As the atmosphere on the dark and stormy winter's night gets eerier and eerier, a noise like a thunderclap is heard, the candle blows out, and all concerned think they have been attacked by a resurrectionist or a spirit. When the chaos subsides, the culprit proves to be an exploding bottle of brown stout.

The trial of Burke and Hare created an entire coffin-full of rumours, prominent among which was the belief that bodysnatchers used covert means to murder victims. Around 1830 a broadside was published on this subject. Entitled *Burking by Means of Snuff*, it told the cautionary tale of one John Wilson, 'a desperate character, and of ferocious countenance', who over several years had murdered many people. His downfall came when he accosted a labourer breaking stones on the road between Lauder and Dalkeith. The man was suspicious of Wilson's insistence, so he had the snuff analysed by a chemist in Dalkeith; it contained arsenic. The police caught Wilson several days later, driving a carriage containing the bodies of three travellers last seen heading towards Lauder. According to the broadside, Wilson was incarcerated at Edinburgh, awaiting trial for murder.

However, John Wilson, the arsenic snuff, and the multiple murders – none of these appear in any legal records. The entire broadside is complete fiction, a classic example of a post-Burke-and-Hare scare story.

FALA
Anecdote only.
Address: Fala Church, Fala, EH37 5SY.
NGR: NT43883 60945.
Lat, Long: 55.838448, -2.897599.
Access: Parking close by. Gravel paths.
Comments: A pleasant church in a small village on the A68.
Stories: On one occasion watchers fired on suspected graverobbers, but in the morning the only victim was the minister's badly-wounded goat. There were at least two cases of actual bodysnatching.

GLENCORSE
The setting for Stevenson's The Body-Snatcher, *included at the end of this book. Fine watch-house.*
Address: Glencorse Old Kirk, at entrance to Glencorse House, between Milton Bridge and Crosshouse, near Penicuik, EH26 0NZ.
NGR: NT24491 63051.
Lat, Long: 55.854717, -3.207753.
Access: The owners are happy to allow access at no charge to those with a genuine interest, as long as it arranged in advance. See www.glencorsehouse.com. Getting in with a wheelchair requires a little work, as the short lane up from the first set of gates to the churchyard gate is very steep. The pedestrian route from Glencorse House passes over a stile.
Things to see: The miniscule watch-house next to the gate became an offertory house after 1832, and is now the toilet block for use during weddings at the kirk.
Comments: The country kirk has been beautifully restored as a wedding venue, and is surrounded by interestingly carved stones.
Stories: Stevenson's short story is a classic horror tale. RLS knew the area well.

Glencorse, the setting for Robert Louis Stevenson's *The Body-Snatcher*, with its tiny watch-house. *(Geoff Holder)*

An excellent caged lair at Lasswade. (*Geoff Holder*)

The Lasswade mortstone for laying atop coffins. (*Geoff Holder*)

LASSWADE

A real treat.

Address: Lasswade Old Kirkyard, Church Road/School Brae, Lasswade, EH18 1NB

NGR: NT30178 66106.

Lat, Long: 55.882977, -3.117569.

Access: The gates are opposite the modern cemetery on a winding uphill lane. Space for three cars. Gravel paths.

Things to see: 1. The medieval church was abandoned after 1793 and its various parts converted into family burial aisles. The site now consists of the roofless nave of the old kirk plus four burial enclosures of various dates. Immediately east of the old church is the caged lair of the Calderwood Enclosure, its large hooped ironwork roof set above its solid stone walls. 2. Just west of the Eldon Aisle is a large vaguely coffin-shaped mortstone. 3. The bell tower stood until 1866, long after the church was abandoned. A solid structure three storeys high, the lower floor was used as a watch-house. The outline of the tower's footprint is set out in the grass.

Comments: Delightful, well-kept old kirkyard with many sculpted stones. Interpretation panels.

Stories: On a freezing cold night in 1829, anatomist John Lizars opened his door and found on his doorstep James Hewit and James Gow, the latter a known counterfeiter and thief. They wanted money for a spade and tools to lift a body. Lizars shut the door on them so they went to another nearby anatomist, Thomas Aitken. He told them he wouldn't give them any money in advance, but if they managed to retrieve the body then he and his brother John would take it. Two nights later Gow and Hewit returned with two more resurrectionists and a woman's corpse in a bag. No questions were asked. The next night, the four were back again, this time with a child. The night after that – with four more resurrectionists in tow – they brought a man. Lizars decided he would also have that one. They were paid for their efforts and no more was said – until there was an outcry in Lasswade.

Helen Miller, a widow from the village, had turned informant. She had come to Edinburgh and met with Hewit, telling him about the bodies in her local kirkyard. There was no night watch, she said: it would be easy pickings for him. When none of the anatomists would advance Hewit the money for tools, Miller even lent him a spade. She was paid for her information. Unfortunately for them, Hewit was not the only person Miller had told about the bodies. Each night that they visited the kirkyard, more and more resurrectionists had shown up. By the third night there had been quite a crowd, all digging up various graves in the hope of finding more fresh corpses. Realising they were creating a bit of a scene and desperate not to get caught, they all departed without refilling the ransacked graves. They'd also left bits of the rejected rotting bodies lying all over the grass. Eight men travelling from a kirkyard to Surgeons' Square with a suspiciously body-shaped bag hadn't gone unnoticed and the Aitkens' premises were searched. The brothers tried to bluff it out, inviting the sister of the dead man (whose body was with Lizars, not with them) to have a good look round. She instantly recognised the bodies of the woman and child from Lasswade. The police needed more than her say so, though. They needed relatives of the deceased to come and formally identify their loved ones. They warned the anatomists they would be back on Monday morning. But when the police and family members arrived, a 'terrible error' had occurred. The Aitkens had 'discovered' that their students had taken the corpses and dissected them without their knowledge. The bodies were no longer recognisable. Such a shame, but these things happen. The case fell apart and the informer, the anatomists and the resurrectionists all got off scot-free.

Gow, however, was soon back in the saddle, paying a caretaker to leave open the death-room of Barbara Rodger in Old Assembly Close. But when he and his companions arrived in the pre-dawn, the door was locked, so he broke it open. This was housebreaking, a serious crime, and when arrested the multiple-offender was sentenced to seven years' transportation. After the trial Robert Knox passed a shilling on to Gow's wife in Blackfriars Wynd, indicating Gow had been a regular supplier.

NEWBATTLE
A lovely site but no bodysnatching remnants remain.
Address: Newbattle Road, Newbattle, Eskbank, EH22 3LQ.
NGR: NT33095 66220.
Lat, Long: 55.883115, -3.070749.
Access: Park in the modern cemetery immediately to the north and either walk along the busy narrow road or go through the small gate in the south wall, which gives out onto the old graveyard. The site is grassy and uneven.
Comments: A lovely old burial-ground, with mature yew trees and numerous carved stones.
Stories: The watch-house used to stand against the east wall. A watcher named Hume fired at three resurrectionists, hitting one in the leg. The trio ran off, one man bleeding profusely. Hume became a local hero, and was presented with a pair of pistols paid for by public subscription.

In 1827 an eccentric elderly woman named Margaret Hawthorn, but known to all as Camp Meg, perished in a snowstorm. She was apparently an educated gentlewoman on the run from a scandal in her youth, and over decades her ability to heal animals, masculine clothes and desire to live alone, had all given her the reputation of being a witch. She had been cared for in her last illness by a local doctor, and apparently sold her body to him in advance, for an upfront payment of £1 and a promise that her remains after dissection would be interred by her beloved hovel on Camp Hill. It appears that none of the post-mortem bargains were honoured, as she was buried without dissection in Newbattle Cemetery on 13 May 1827. No stone remains to mark the spot of her last resting place.

NEWTON
A watch-house and bullet-marked stone.

Address: Newton Church, Newton Church Road, Newton Village, EH22 1SR (near Danderhall, Edinburgh).

NGR: NT31497 69299.

Lat, Long: 55.912273, -3.098049.

Access: Tarmac paths.

Things to see: 1. The watch-house by the Windy Gow entrance was built around 1828. It is in good condition but the chimney has been removed and the windows blocked-up. It now houses the gravedigger's equipment. 2. One of the vertical slabs propped up by a metal bar bears the mark of a watcher's bullet.

Comments: Some fine carved stones.

Stories: Jock or Johnny Blyth, a local vagrant, fell asleep at Newton, only to be woken by a cart arriving, and then two men climbing the wall. The weather was bad and the horse restless, so when the corpse was lifted one man said he would go and calm the animal. At this point a voice issued from beneath a table tombstone: 'I'll gang oot an' haud the horse for you.' Faced with the apparent literal resurrection of the dead, the two bodysnatchers turned tail and fled, leaving behind the cadaver – and a valuable horse and cart.

OLD PENTLAND
A fine watch-house.

Address: Pentland Old Cemetery, Old Pentland, Pentland Road, near Loanhead, EH20 9NU.

NGR: NT26240 66331.

Lat, Long: 55.884305, -3.180397.

Access: Through a kissing gate and up a grassy slope to the main gates. On the north side of a busy road, with no parking. It is less than a mile's walk from the mega-car park of the Ikea store on the A720.

Things to see: The tiny watch-house at the gate can be entered and its features investigated – a fireplace, a small barred window, and barely enough room for two or three people. It also stores a pair of medieval stones.

Comments: A pocket country churchyard with many carved gravestones. Interpretation panels.

Stories: In 1742 – in one of the earliest cases of bodysnatching – gardener John Samuel took a child's body from Pentland. He was caught red-handed at the Potterow Port city gates in Edinburgh, and consequently whipped through the streets of the city and banished from Scotland for seven years.

PENICUIK
Anecdote only.

Address: St Mungo's Church, Kirkhill Road/ High Street, Penicuik, EH26 8JB.

NGR: NT23729 59990.

Lat, Long: 55.827091, -3.219059.

Access: Parking in front of the church. Good paved paths.

Comments: The ruins of the old St Kentigern's Church nestle attractively in the graveyard behind the present parish church.

Stories: The notorious Edinburgh bodysnatcher Andrew Lees or Merrilees had a sister who died in Penicuik. Filled with fraternal devotion, he resolved to lift her body and sell it. Two of his confederates, 'Spoon' (a deaf-mute) and Mowatt (known as 'Moudewart', meaning 'mole') believed he had bilked them out of 10s on a recent snatch, and so resolved to pre-empt Lees and steal the body themselves. Ah, honour amongst thieves. The two men procured a donkey and cart and started to rifle the grave after midnight. Once the body was lifted, there came a shout, and from behind a tombstone rose a fearful white-robed figure with extended arms. The terrified duo jumped into the cart and fled. At which point Andrew Lees, having got his erstwhile colleagues to do the hard labour for him, removed the ghostly white sheet, wrapped his sister's body in it, and set off to Edinburgh. Before long he gained sight of the hapless duo, and by dint of shouting 'Stop thief!' forced them to abandon the cart. So the cunning Mr Lees made his comfortable way to the city, where a satisfactory transaction took place at Surgeons' Square. Lees was a career criminal (housebreaking and theft) with a distinctive physiognomy and a known address in Scott's

Close off the Cowgate, but whenever the heat was on he simply left Edinburgh until the police lost interest, and thus was never arrested for any crime. In the second volume of his *Psychic Investigators Casebook*, Archibald Lawrie, Secretary of the Scottish Society for Psychical Research, reported a medium's encounter with the spirit of Andrew Lees in a former doctor's residence in Edinburgh's New Town.

The Watching Committee bought a pair of guns and built a watch-house along the northern wall of the kirkyard at a cost of £20 (it was demolished in 1870). The watch was usually kept by two men, and continued until the late year of 1840. One night Henry Dewar imagined he heard bodysnatchers at work, and fired into the darkness. There was a hit, and there was blood, but let's just say that the next day, pork chops were on the menu...

In his pre-murder days William Burke lodged in the High Street while working as a labourer on the construction of the mill-lade for the paper mill.

🂠 🂠 🂠 🂠 🂠 🂠 🂠 🂠 🂠 🂠 🂠 🂠 🂠 🂠 🂠 🂠 🂠

WEST LOTHIAN
ABERCORN
Anecdote only, excellent site otherwise.
Address: Abercorn Church, Abercorn, EH30 9SL.
NGR: NT08141 79097.
Lat, Long: 55.991450, -3.452567.
Access: Signposted from the A904, then along walled drive from the village. Mostly good paths, some slopes.
Comments: An architecturally wonderful church, superb symbolic gravestones among mature trees, and a terrific collection of early carved stones in the tiny museum within the gatehouse.
Stories: On Saturday 21 February 1820, a stranger approached several people in Abercorn asking for different sets of directions. On Sunday morning, as the villagers gathered for divine service, someone noticed that the grave of a recently-buried child had been disturbed. The coffin was dug up in front of the entire congregation, and found to be empty. An angry search party set out, and soon located the missing shroud, cast into a ditch on the Queensferry road. The landlord of Hallidays inn stated that two men had arrived the previous night in a chaise. They left the driver sleeping, while they went out late, only returning at 3 a.m., after which they departed for Edinburgh. While at the inn they had met with the stranger seen on the previous day, who was later identified as John Herron. Herron was questioned by the authorities but denied he had been in the area on that Saturday. A week later John and his brother Andrew were implicated in the incident at Scotlandwell (see the Perth & Kinross chapter).

BATHGATE
Anecdote only.
Address: Gideon Street, Bathgate EH48 4HB.
NGR: NS97555 69115.
Lat, Long: 55.904205, -3.640152.
Access: Some steps.
Comments: A substantial church in a city-centre location.
Stories: When Thomas Dennis' child was lifted, the snatchers ineptly left the shroud draped over the grave. Suspicion fell on a man named Wilson, who was thus forced to quit the town. When a prominent local man, James Reid of The Glen, was buried, it was known that his body would become a target, and a watch was successfully kept for several weeks. In 1902 the *Linlithgowshire Journal & Gazette* interviewed ninety-year-old David Alexander, who recalled being employed as a watcher at the High Church for 1s 6d per night (doing a shift at the Old Parish Church at Kirkton attracted an extra 6d). 'I had always an old gun with me while on duty at the kirkyards, but though anyone came, what could I do? – naething.'

ECCLESMACHAN

An extraordinary anecdote and a stained-glass window.

Address: Ecclesmachan (Strathbrock) Parish Church, Ecclesmachan, EH52 6NJ (on the B8046 north of Uphall).

NGR: NT05882 73663.

Lat, Long: 55.946755, -3.508605.

Access: The old graveyard is grassed and slightly uneven.

Things to see: The upper circular stained-glass window in the west wall of the church is a memorial to Dr Robert Liston.

Comments: Splendid gravestones.

Stories: Sometime in the 1920s or 1930s, a workman was repairing the roof of Ecclesmachan Manse when he fell through the timbers. Fortunately he was unhurt, having landed in an attic that had long been closed off. As he sat up, recovering his senses, he found himself sitting right next to a skeleton. The bones were not recent. Circumstantial evidence, therefore, links the skeleton to a son of the manse, Robert Liston. Robert was the eldest son of Revd Henry Liston, minister of Ecclesmachan from 1793 until 1836. He grew up to be a physically powerful young man with a grip of steel and an unerring eye, talents which proved of great value in the days of surgery without anaesthesia. In later years Liston was one of the most prominent surgeons of his day, fêted for his innovations and for performing the first major operation using ether to keep the patient unconscious. He was also an enthusiastic bodysnatcher, often leading his students on raids. His exploits are described in the sections on Rosyth and Culross (Fife) and Drummond Street (Edinburgh). It is likely the skeleton was a relic of those days, although why Liston hid it in his father's attic will forever remain a mystery. The human remains finally found some dignity when they were buried in the churchyard.

KIRKLISTON

A mortsafe and a watch-house.

Address: Parish Church, The Square, Bowling Green Road, Kirkliston, EH29 9AX.

NGR: NT12511 74367.

Lat, Long: 55.954259, -3.403163.

Access: Five steps up from the street. Tarmac paths and grass.

Things to see: 1. A rusted iron horizontal gate-like mortsafe lies embedded in low stones surrounding a lair. 2. The watch-house beside the gate is in good condition, with boarded-up windows and a tall chimneystack.

Comments: The charming church lies in the heart of the village.

Stories: In 1818 two bodies were taken, leading the Kirk Session to offer a reward of £20 for information on the perpetrators. Despite the size of the sum, and advertisements being circulated in three newspapers, no-one came forward. The graveyard thereafter was watched after funerals. In December 1818, watchmen on duty in cold weather were granted the boon of a loaf of bread and a glass of spirits. On a night two years later, the watchers broke several windows in the church. The incident was poorly reported – could the Session have been embarrassed by the drunken antics of their employees?

LINLITHGOW

A good mortsafe.

Address: St Michael's Parish Church, Kirkgate, Linlithgow, EH49 7AL.

NGR: NT00235 77284.

Lat, Long: 55.766887, 3.600357.

Access: Car park on site. The graveyard has decent paths and some steps.

Things to see: The Linlithgow Mortsafe Society was founded on 19 February 1819. The partially-broken lid of a mortsafe lies in the Livingston Burial Vault, south-east of the church. The iron box on which it was mounted has not survived. The lid was held in place by a flange at one end and then screwed down at the other.

Comments: Justly described as the finest parish church in Scotland, St Michael's has the grandeur of a miniature cathedral. Linlithgow Palace (cared for by Historic Scotland) is next door.

Stories: The first cadaver known to have been stolen from Linlithgow was that of Benjamin Jamieson or Davidson. The trail of the snatchers was followed over the soft ground of the Peel to the Duke's Entry, where a carriage had presumably been waiting. When a second body was stolen it was pointed out that the man had not been a member of the Mortsafe Society and thus his grave had not been protected. The watch-house (erected in 1823, now gone) stood against the south wall of the churchyard. Three men were on duty per night, and each householder attended twice a year, or had to provide a substitute.

For Linlithgow's dramatic intervention in the Larbert body-thefts of 1823, see the Falkirk chapter. On another occasion two historical-minded American visitors, presumably ignorant of the prevailing tensions, were looking round the church after nightfall, mistaken for resurrection-men, and assaulted by the mob.

RATHO

A ruined watch-house.

Address: Parish Church, Baird Road, Ratho, EH28 8NP.

NGR: NT13848 71005.

Lat, Long: 55.924369, -3.380249.

Access: Parking at the front. Level access to graveyard past the offertory house at the entrance.

Things to see: The utterly ruined watch-house is badly overgrown and inaccessible.

Comments: A pleasing spot with some interesting gravestones.

TORPHICHEN

An offertory house used as a watch-house.

Address: Torphichen Preceptory and Parish Church, Bowyett, Torphichen, EH48 4LZ.

NGR: NS96884 72518.

Lat, Long: 55.93461, -3.652181.

Access: Parking outside. Good quality paths. The Preceptory is open on weekends 1 p.m. to 5 p.m. from 1 April to 30 September. Admission charge. The kirkyard is open at all reasonable times.

Things to see: The windowless offertory house at the entrance to the right of the car park was temporarily used by the watchmen until a purpose-built watch-house was erected in the centre of the churchyard. This latter watch-house has since been swept away.

Comments: Although extensively altered, it is still possible to breathe the atmosphere of the Middle Ages here.

UPHALL

A watchers' window.

Address: Uphall Church, Ecclesmachan Road, Uphall, EH52 6JP.

NGR: NT05981 72211.

Lat, Long: 55.933733, -3.506514.

Access: Well-laid paths, parking close by.

Things to see: Immediately above the Romanesque arched doorway in the south wall of the church is a circular window. This, it is claimed, was where a woman sat night after night, a loaded gun ready to make sure that any would-be bodysnatchers had a visit to remember. Why this uncomfortable and inaccessible perch, when there are other places where a guard could have been maintained?

Comments: A fine church bursting with architectural and historic interest.

Stories: The Uphall Society For The Preservation of The Dead was formed in November 1822, charging 6d entry money and the same annual fee thereafter. The money was used to buy large mortstones to cover freshly-made graves.

GLASGOW AND THE WEST

'Who is not made better and wiser by occasional intercourse with the tomb?'
George Blair, *Biographic and Descriptive Sketches of the Glasgow Necropolis*

GLASGOW

Glasgow was Edinburgh's great rival in medical education. In 1801 there were ninety students of anatomy registered at the university, more than 200 every year between 1809 and 1814, with an extraordinary peak of 352 in 1813. From 1824 to 1829 the annual number again exceeded 200, dropping after that date. In addition to these students at the official university, there were many dozens attending private anatomy schools run by talented and ambitious surgeons who worked outside the university system. Many corpses were harvested illegally in Ireland, but by and large the Irish 'subjects' were bought up by the university, leaving the private anatomy schools to find their own sources.

ANDERSTON
Anecdote only.
Address: Under the M8!
NGR: NS57 65.
Lat, Long: 55.85, -4.26.
Comments: Most of Anderston, including the burial-ground, was wiped out when the motorway was built.
Stories: At three o'clock in the morning of 17 March 1828, the night watch disturbed four men behaving suspiciously near the graveyard. The only one caught was former gravedigger Henry Gillies, an unsavoury character who had lost his job for stealing grave furniture, and had been banned from Anderston because he was observed at funerals checking the depth of the new graves. Gillies was sentenced to nine months' imprisonment for violating a sepulchre. Just before he was caught he had dumped the bodies of a poor elderly woman and of Margaret McNeil, a young child who had succumbed to whooping cough. Margaret's distraught mother was a poverty-stricken widow, and her plight attracted much sympathy, so a woman from a higher social class offered to rebury the little girl alongside her own recently deceased child. In a shocking development, the lair was opened, only to reveal that the body of the second little girl had also been taken.

BEARSDEN
No visible remains, but nice site.
Address: New Kilpatrick Parish Church, 28 Kirk Place, Bearsden, G61 3RT.
NGR: NS54341 72276.
Lat, Long: 55.921442, -4.332501.
Access: Good access to the large well-kept graveyard. Parking.
Stories: In October 1832 watchmen fired on a party of bodysnatchers. The following morning at 5 a.m. Dr Carlaw was found dead on the path to his house in Maryhill, and the funeral was hastily arranged before the body could be examined. The good doctor may have been on the raid.

BLACKFRIARS/HIGH STREET
Anecdote only.
Address: High Street, Glasgow, G1 1PP.
NGR: NS5988 6509.
Lat, Long: 55.858619, -4.240142.
Comments: The church and graveyard of Blackfriars on the east side of High Street are long gone.
Stories: A medical student was killed by a trip-gun here. His two horrified companions

tied each of his legs to one of theirs and staggered back home, pretending to be a typical group of drunken students. The dead man was put to bed in his lodgings, and the next day the rumour was put about that he had committed suicide with a gun. The other two resurrectionists were therefore safe from opprobrium, and it was only years later that the true story came out.

The search for a woman's body lifted in July 1827 resulted in the discovery of the corpse hidden in a box addressed to John Hamilton, 9 Prince's Street, Edinburgh. In March 1832 three men attempted to steal the body of a young boy as it lay out at the actual wake. They were interrupted as they left the apartment on High Street, and fled without their booty.

BRIDGETON

Anecdote only.
Address: Tullis Street Memorial Garden, Bridgeton, Glasgow, G40 1HW.
NGR: NS6061 6372.
Lat, Long: 55.846530, 55.846530.
Access: Level paths.
Comment: The graveyard on Tullis Street (formerly John Street) was closed in 1870 and the bodies exhumed. After recent regeneration the grassed area is now a memorial garden.
Stories: In December 1823 a family suffered a double tragedy: one child died, followed shortly by a sibling. When the first grave was opened to accommodate the second child, the coffin was found to be empty. The horror prompted citizens to patrol the graveyard armed with pistols and swords, which created its own tragedy when a young man protecting his sister's grave was accidentally killed by his own weapon. The following year the Bridgeton Grave Protecting Society was founded, with a fundraising song composed by Radical poet Alexander Rodger:

Ye who mourn dear friends departed,
By the hand of death laid low;
Ye who, lone and broken-hearted,
Secretly indulge your woe:

'Mid your plaintive sighs and wailings,
One sad comfort, now, you have,
Shock'd no more shall be your feelings,
O'er a plundered, empty grave.

Midnight prowlers bent on robbing,
Shall no more your dead molest;
Now, 'the wicked cease from troubling,'
Now, 'the weary are at rest:'
Soundly sleeps your sire or mother,
Faithful husband, virtuous wife,
Son or daughter, sister, brother,
Safe from the dissector's knife.

O'er the hallowed green turf kneeling,
Shedding fond affection's tear,
Soothed will be your every feeling,
With, 'Thy dear-loved dust' lies here;
Here, too, shalt thou long repose thee,
In the calm and peaceful tomb,
Till the Archangel's trump shall rouse thee,
Radiant with immortal bloom.

BROOMIELAW

Anecdote only.
Address: Broomielaw, Glasgow, G1 4RLL
NGR: NS58 64.
Lat, Long: 55.856, -4.267.
Access: Street in city centre.
Comments: This fashionable riverside area was once a major quay for small to medium-sized vessels.
Stories: In 1812 an Irish sloop unloaded a batch of packages described as 'linen rags' to a shed on Broomielaw. There the cargo lay unclaimed for several days, at which point the smell was so bad that the packages were opened to reveal a clutch of bodies – men, women and children. In 1828 a box burst open as it was being transferred from a steamer to a cart on the dockside, and a human foot was revealed protruding from the packaging. The police took charge of the package, but nothing could be found about the sender or recipient, as it was merely marked 'to be called for'. The body was therefore quietly and decently interred.

CALTON

Anecdote only.

Address: Calton Old Graveyard, 309-341 Abercromby Street, Calton, Glasgow, G40 2NB.

NGR: NS60543 64205.

Lat, Long: 55.850819, -4.229180.

Access: Easy pedestrian and reasonable wheelchair access.

Comments: Historically interesting small cemetery, a bit decrepit.

Stories: The Calton burgh police force was set up in 1819, the area considered so dangerous that the men were issued with cutlasses. A pair of officers took on a bodysnatcher at Abercromby Street and severed his arm above the elbow. It is not recorded whether the individual then tried to interest an anatomist in purchasing the supernumerary limb ('It's fresh, guv, honest! Look, you can see the cutmarks!') In 1827 a destitute young Irishman died in Calton, and after he had been waked and was on his way to the burial-ground, his drunken uncle attacked the funeral party, telling them he needed to sell the body of his nephew to the anatomists, crying 'Have I not a right to make as much of it as I can?' He was heavily fined.

In February 1829, following the Burke and Hare trial, Margaret Logue walked from Edinburgh to Glasgow, carrying her infant daughter in her arms and sleeping by roadsides and in hayricks. She lodged anonymously in Calton, staying indoors during the day and creeping out to Broomielaw at dawn and twilight to find a steamer to take her to Ireland. On the fourth or fifth day she was recognised by a drunken woman in Clyde Street, who shouted out, 'Hare's wife! – burke her!' Attacked by the crowd, Logue fled to Calton, but was still being beaten when the police arrived and she was placed in custody for her own protection.

The *Glasgow Chronicle* described her condition: 'She seemed to be completely overcome, and occasionally bursting into tears she bewailed her unhappy situation, which she declared had been brought about by Hare's profligacy. All she desired was to get across the channel to Ireland, where she hoped to end her days in some remote spot near her native place, where she would live in retirement and penitence. As for Hare, she would never live with him again.' This was a bit rich coming from someone who had a definite hand in several of the murders. By this point a riot was imminent. She was kept in a cell for two nights, and then spirited out of the country on the steamer *Fingal*, bound for Belfast via Greenock, and the utmost secrecy was required during the voyage to ensure her safety.

CARMUNNOCK

Regulations for the Watch.

Address: Kirk Road/Busby Road, Carmunnock, G76 9BY.

NGR: NS59912 57487.

Lat, Long: 55.790321, -4.235788.

Access: Park in the village. Bus #31 from Glasgow or East Kilbride. Main path is paved.

Things to see: The small watch-house by the gate has the painted set of Regulations for the Watch, dated 1828. Watchmen had to be on duty from an hour after sunset to daybreak and were prohibited from getting drunk, leaving the churchyard during the duty hours, or admitting visitors who did not give the password. 'They Are Also Prohibited from Making Noise, Or Firing Guns, Except When There is Cause of Alarm that Any of the Inhabitants in Such Cases May be Able to turn Out to the Assistance of the Watch'. The final regulation warns watchers they will be financially liable for any damage they cause. The watch-house is kept locked: to see the board, visit on a Saturday between April and September when guides are on site between 2-4 p.m.

Comments: A lovely site in a conservation village, well worth visiting.

CATHCART

A caged lair and a shattered watch-house.

Address: Old Cathcart Parish Church, 118-120 Carmunnock Road, Cathcart,

Glasgow, G44 5UH (opposite the current kirk, also confusingly called Old Cathcart Parish Church).
NGR: NS58726 60618.
Lat, Long: 55.818086, -4.256312.
Access: The gates are permanently locked.
Things to see: 1. A large and elaborate anti-bodysnatching iron cage, viewable from Carmunnock Road. 2. A tiny roofless watch-house, the rear of which juts out into Kilmailing Road from the graveyard wall. It had a fireplace and a single window.
Comments: The site is dominated by the derelict tower of the former church. Vandalism is much in evidence.

The 'animal cage' iron bars around a lair at Cathcart Old Parish Church. *(Geoff Holder)*

CLYDE STREET
Anecdote only.
Address: Clyde Street, Glasgow centre, G1 4LH.
NGR: NS5916 6472.
Lat, Long: 55.855087, -4.251443.
Stories: A fine eighteenth-century mansion once stood at the junction of Clyde Street and Ropework Lane. It was reportedly haunted by its first owner, the wealthy merchant Robert Dreghorn, often called 'the ugliest man in Glasgow'. 'Bob Dragon' had committed suicide in 1806, and apart from one tenant – who left in a hurry – the house remained empty until George Provand, an oil and colour merchant, took it at a knockdown rent. One fateful Saturday night in February 1822 a group of post-pub revellers peeped through the windows of the 'haunted house' and saw two severed heads pooled in blood. By the following afternoon a mob was breaking down the door and plundering the removables. Pursued by cries of 'bodysnatcher' and 'murderer', the elderly Provand fled for his life. In fact, what the drunken idiots had seen was two large jars of black paint in a spill of red pigment. Dragoons and infantry with drawn bayonets quelled the riot. The ringleaders got fourteen years' transportation, or, if they were lucky, a whipping through the city streets. Dreghorn's mansion has long been replaced by a warehouse.

COLLEGE STREET
Major historical site, but no visible remains.
Address: College Street, Glasgow centre, G1 1QH.
NGR: NS5977 6521.
Lat, Long: 55.859664, -4.241960.
Access: Street in city centre.
Comments: Urban development has removed all traces of the notorious anatomy schools.
Stories: Before the university relocated to the more salubrious West End, the area around College Street and High Street held several anatomy schools, one within the university itself, others privately funded. The kirkyards of Ramshorn, Blackfriars and the cathedral were all within walking distance – or body-carrying distance. Of course, being in the city centre meant that the university was handy for any mob inflamed by the resurrectionist outrage *du jour*. There were attacks in the 1740s, in January 1803 and March 1823. In the latter two cases the college buildings had to be protected from assault by armed troops.

Following the Ramshorn scandals of 1813, the university authorities had prohibitions on stealing bodies read out at the start of the academic session, warning that any student guilty of such misconduct would be expelled. A similar edict was enforced two years later. (All this probably had the effect of pushing the more ardent student anatomists towards the private schools.)

In 1805 John Burns, founder of the first College Street private anatomy school, was banned from teaching anatomy because of his involvement in a bodysnatching case. His replacement was his twenty-four-year-old brother Allan, a brilliant surgeon who later wrote several pioneering anatomical textbooks. In 1809 Allan appointed as his assistant and demonstrator Dr Granville Sharp Pattison. When Allan died in 1813, Pattison went into business with surgeon Andrew Russel. Peter Mackenzie's *Reminiscences of Glasgow* energetically described the culture of the twenty or thirty students who cleaved to the young Pattison and his advocacy of body-theft as the route to understanding anatomy: 'a band of whom a sacred bond of brotherhood was entered into, that they would not divulge any of their anatomy secrets out of their own closets, nor betray each other under any circumstances whatever. They secretly hired a suite of rooms for the purpose of their anatomy proceedings in the neighbourhood of College Street; each of them had a private key to that anatomy den... these medical students would meet in their quiet haunts in College Street, and draw lots for lifting the body from the grave.'

GLASGOW CATHEDRAL

Large site, with many anecdotes and a few things to see.
Address: Castle Street, Glasgow centre, G4 0UZ.
NGR: NS60255 65657.
Lat, Long: 55.862852, -4.235655.
Access: Pedestrian and reasonable wheelchair access off Castle Street and Cathedral Square.
Things to see: Several large iron cages around graves. One is dated 1840.
Comments: The magnificent Glasgow Cathedral is cared for by Historic Scotland and open to visitors. The grounds are extensive and contain many elaborate carved monuments.

A caged lair at Glasgow Cathedral. *(Geoff Holder)*

Stories: The anatomists' rooms were hard by, so this, the largest graveyard in old Glasgow, was a frequent target. In 1803 the magistrates offered a reward of 20 guineas for information on the theft of a woman's body. Twenty years later, medical student Alexander McGowan was caught lifting the corpse of weaver Thomas Seggie, and was beaten unconscious, with a riot following. McGowan skipped bail and home fled to Ireland, so he was outlawed. Other dutiful citizens surprised a trio of resurrectionists in the graveyard – two fled, but nineteen-year-old John Carmichael was nabbed and charged with violating the sepulchre of building worker John Dempster. The case was never brought to trial – probably because Carmichael's parents paid the Dempsters not to pursue the case. A watch was sometimes kept, a pistol being fired at midnight to give notice that firearms were present and graverobbers could be met with lethal force.

A young surgeon who ran one of the private schools had wanted to conduct a postmortem examination on someone who had died of a baffling disease, but was rebuffed by the relatives. Suspecting an attempt would be made to lift the body, the family hired watchmen for a 24-hour vigil. On the first evening the guards set up a darkened lantern on the grave, its light only shining in their direction, where they lay hidden behind other gravestones. Late at night the lantern was seen to quiver, so one of the watchers fired his gun – scattering the three or four resurrectionists. A few days later the surgeon died of an infection, allegedly caused by a slip of the scalpel, but possibly from a bullet wound.

The urban legend of the 'undead corpse' has an outing here. Two weavers employed as watchmen spotted a pair of resurrectionists stuffing a body into a sack. The graverobbers briefly left to check that the coast was clear, so one of the weavers changed places with the corpse and was soon hoisted onto a brawny shoulder. The bodysnatcher then asked his companion which way they should go, at which point the weaver grabbed the man by the hair and croaked in ghastly tones, 'Doon the Rottonrow, ye scoundrel!' According to Robert Alison's *The Anecdotage of Glasgow*, 'The sack was instantly dropped, and it is said the bearer of it went mad with fright.'

GOVAN

No visible remains.
Address: Govan Old Parish Church, 868 Govan Road, Govan, Glasgow, G51 3AQ.
NGR: NS55349 65917.
Lat, Long: 55.864658, -4.312985.
Access: Good pedestrian and reasonable wheelchair access.
Comments: Fascinating old graveyard. Some vandalism.
Stories: A team of students were disturbed just as they were about to prise open the coffin. All escaped, but one could only do so by swimming across the River Clyde to the north shore. In later life he became an eminent physician and surgeon.

MARYHILL

Anecdote only.
Address: Corner of Maryhill Road and Duart Street, Maryhill, G20 0EG.
NGR: NS56280 69562.
Lat, Long: 55.897652, -4.30004.
Access: Permanently locked.
Comments: Maryhill Old Church has been demolished. The overgrown graveyard can be

viewed through the bars. The watch-house has vanished.
Stories: The church was built in 1825. Two years later, when there were as yet very few interments in the kirkyard, the body of Mrs Purdon was taken. The local doctor, James Carlaw, had a bit too much to drink one night and told some friends that Granny Purdon's corpse had been concealed on Gilshochill before being carried to the anatomist's table. He also passed round a 'lifting' spade (for more on Dr Carlaw, see Bearsden). Shortly afterwards the body of a child was found in a field on Gilshochill – it had been taken from Maryhill kirkyard and stashed there pending the opportunity to deliver the prize to the anatomy school. Suspicion fell upon a well-known local thief and roustabout, but nothing was proved (he eventually served a sentence of fourteen years' transportation for robbery).

As a result of these depredations, a watch-house was put up at the south-west corner of the kirkyard and a number of young men took turns patrolling at night. Local man Alexander Thomson left a memoir of this period. By and large, the duties were not taken all that seriously, as the lads took the opportunity to raid the local henhouses and gardens for food, and use their watching allowance to buy booze. Their girlfriends also turned up to help pass the time. During the winter of 1831-32, two youths were on guard duty when one, J.D., decided to play a practical joke on his nervous companion J.L. The anxious youth was walking the grounds at midnight, carrying his gun loaded with 'sparrow hail' – small particles used to shoot birds – when he heard spitting and growling noises coming from a large flat tombstone, while a pair of feet emerged from under the slab. J.L. cried, 'Be ye devil or ghost, here's at ye,' fired the gun and bolted out of the gate, sprinting through the unlit streets until the terror finally left him. He managed to rouse a sleeping friend and, fortified by each other's presence, the duo crept warily back into the graveyard – where they found J.D. 'with his trousers riddled, and his legs pock-marked and fern-speckled by the sparrow hail'.

THE NECROPOLIS

Amazing site with a couple of items related to our quest.

Address: off Cathedral Square, Glasgow centre, G4 0YB.

NGR: NS6010 6524.

Lat, Long: 55.862163, -4.233166.

Access: Main entrance off Cathedral Square at the elaborate wrought-iron gates. Other entrances off Wishart Street. Reasonable wheelchair access to some parts but many slopes. The Friends of the Glasgow Necropolis organise popular walking tours (see www.glasgownecropolis.org.)

Things to see: 1. The Catacombs. 2. The tomb of Dr Pattison. 3. A single low iron mortsafe, its diamond lattice-work upper surface overgrown with vegetation. Several other lattice-work mortsafes have been found at ground level but were re-covered.

Comments: A true city of the dead, this vast and grandiose nineteenth-century spectacle of sculpture is as theatrical as graveyards get, with monuments of every architectural fashion. Some vandalism, and the site is often home to the intoxicated.

Stories: The Necropolis was a grand scheme designed to replace the increasingly overcrowded and fetid old parish graveyards at Govan, Cathcart, Rutherglen, Shettleston, Tollcross and the cathedral. When it was designed, bodysnatching was still a threat, so a subterranean morthouse system was constructed, with six private burial vaults and catacombs lined with numerous tiers for holding coffins. A vast tunnel was to be driven through the hill. But the Necropolis opened in 1832, the very year of the Anatomy Act. The catacombs mouldered unused, suffering flooding and eventual abandonment. Their entrance is the first thing you see as you pass from the gates over the Bridge of Sighs above Wishart Street into the Necropolis proper – it is the impressive semi-circular entrance façade directly in front of you.

The façade of the catacombs at the Necropolis. *(Geoff Holder)*

Dr Granville Sharp Pattison, the anatomist at the centre of the Janet McAllister case (see Ramshorn kirkyard, below), is buried in the division of the Necropolis known as Beta, which is on the slope above and east of the catacombs entrance. The family enclosure is particularly impressive, the Pattisons being high achievers, and his is the right-hand tombstone of two matching memorials with family crests. His middle name is misspelt on the stone as 'Sharpe'.

OLD WYND

Anecdote only.

Address: Off Trongate, Glasgow centre, G1 4RY.

NGR: NS5932 6487.

Lat, Long: 55.856480, -4.248967.

Access: Narrow lane off busy pedestrian thoroughfare in city centre.

Stories: This is another sighting of the 'bodysnatchers as murderers' legend. Sinister men toting pads soaked in chloroform lurked in Old Wynd and the adjacent lanes, ready to abduct, kill and sell unsuspecting passers-by. In his book *The Heart of Glasgow*, published in 1972, Jack House recalled meeting elderly people who described how their parents had told them never to pass the wynd entrance at night without first putting their hands over their mouths.

PEOPLE'S PALACE MUSEUM
Address: Glasgow Green, Glasgow, G40 1AT.
NGR: NS60041 64277.
Lat, Long: 55.851309, -4.23722.
Access: Open 10 a.m. to 5 p.m. Tuesday to Thursday and Saturday, and 11 a.m. to 5 p.m. on Friday and Sunday. Closed Mondays. Disabled parking on site, full wheelchair access. Entrance free.
Comments: A truly wonderful museum of Glaswegian social history and ephemera.
Things to see: A mortsafe, probably from Ramshorn kirkyard.

RAMSHORN KIRKYARD
Major Site.
Address: 98 Ingram Street, Glasgow centre, G1 1ES
NGR: NS59598 65289.
Lat, Long: 55.860158, -4.244869.
Access: Good wheelchair access.
Comments: A lovely and (usually) peaceful oasis in the heart of the city. This was once a fashionable burying place for the merchant class.
Things to see: 1. A stone on the west wall dedicated to the McGrigors, the family name of Mrs McAllister; she was buried here, possibly even twice. 2. Several tall iron cages surrounding family lairs.
Stories: One of Glasgow's most notorious bodysnatching episodes occurred on 13 December 1813. A policeman reported seeing two bodysnatchers fleeing in the direction of College Street. The next morning the moneyed classes of the Merchant City were out in force – and soon one tomb was found empty. It belonged to Janet McAllister, the wife of a well-known wool merchant in Hutcheson. A mob quickly formed, its first target being the house of Dr James Jeffrey, the Professor of Anatomy at the university, who suffered his windows being stove in – although subsequent events showed that he was entirely innocent. Police officers, armed with a search-warrant, next entered the rooms of Dr Granville Sharp Pattison in College Street, and after something of a hit-and-miss search, eventually uncovered a jawbone with several teeth still attached, some fingers, and other body parts. Accompanying the cops were the dead woman's brothers, James and Donald McGrigor – both wealthy and powerful merchants – along with her dentist. The latter identified the teeth as those he himself had fitted into Janet McAllister's mouth, and then one of the brothers positively stated that one of the severed fingers once bore his sister's wedding ring. Pattison and his companions were arrested and in classic 'house of horror' fashion, the police later found numerous body parts hidden under the floorboards.

The grisly evidence was placed in sealed glass bottles and at the subsequent trial in Edinburgh on 6 June 1814 presented as 'productions' (the Scottish legal term for items displayed in court). Given the number and nature of the productions, it seemed a foregone conclusion that Pattison and his co-accused – Andrew Russel, his lecturer on surgery, and medical students Robert Munro and John McLean – would be found guilty. But the defence had an ace up their sleeves – the quartet were charged with violating the sepulchre of Mrs McAllister, yet forensic tests showed that none of the body parts on display actually belonged to that person. So, although the defendants had clearly violated a sepulchre somewhere, they were technically innocent of the specific charges against them. Two were acquitted, while Pattison and one of the students received a 'not proven' verdict. So strong was public rancour that Pattison promptly emigrated to the United States, where he founded anatomy departments in Philadelphia and New York, and proceeded to have an illustrious career. Meanwhile, the body parts found in the anatomy rooms were given a second funeral in the McGrigor family lair.

An alternative view of the case was expounded by author Ted Ramsey in his book *Don't Walk Down College Street*. In his

A secure iron framework around a lair in Ramshorn kirkyard. *(Geoff Holder)*

view, Pattison was set up as a victim of a conspiracy. He suggests that many bodies were never buried at all, and simply sold direct to the anatomists. The gravediggers and undertakers thus pocketed two fees – one for the corpse, and the other the minimal fee the council paid for paupers' funerals. This was obviously a nice little earner, but possibly Pattison, the new boy in town, refused to play ball. Ramsey suggests that Pattison chose not to pay the high prices demanded for bodies, and set about acquiring his subjects cheaply himself, encouraging his own students to raid the cathedral graveyard. As revenge, the rebuffed cartel smashed open the tomb of a prominent citizen and laid a false trail that led to Pattison's door. Ramsey's take on the events is an untestable hypothesis, but it remains an intriguing possibility.

Even if the conspiracy angle is false, the 'second funeral' was a sham, because, as the defence counsel showed, Mrs McAllister's body was never in Pattison's sanguinary salon. Her corpse may have been whisked away to another anatomy school. Two bodies had been stolen from the cathedral graveyard a few days previously, and it is likely that the organs and limbs piously buried at the second interment came from these individuals.

SALTMARKET
Anecdote only.
Address: Saltmarket, Glasgow, G1 5LE.
NGR: NS595647.

Lat, Long: 55.854969, -4.245588.
Stories: In August 1828 a poor woman was delivered of a child. That evening her neighbours peeked through a hole in the flimsy partition wall and saw the woman's medical attendant making a parcel of the newborn and placing it underneath his coat. The man was attacked by a mob and taken into custody by the police. On examination, the infant was found to have been still-born, and soon the truth of the matter came out. The student had treated the woman for free: when her child was born dead, she gifted him the body *in lieu* of payment.

SHETTLESTON
A pair of sentry boxes.
Address: Old Shettleston Road, Shettleston, Glasgow, G32 7XW.
NGR: NS6407 964151.
Lat, Long: 55.851344, -4.172718.
Access: Caution required.
Things to see: Two stone 'sentry boxes' on either side of the entrance.
Comments: The church has been demolished, and the graveyard is badly vandalised.
Stories: In 1830 a young girl was buried in a locked mortsafe. The bodysnatchers used a duplicate key and made away with the body.

🦇 🦇 🦇 🦇 🦇 🦇 🦇 🦇 🦇 🦇 🦇 🦇 🦇 🦇 🦇 🦇

RENFREWSHIRE
EAGLESHAM
A watch-house.
Address: Eaglesham Parish Church, Montgomery Street, Eaglesham, G76 0AS.
NGR: NS57232 51819.
Lat, Long: 55.738650, -4.275525.
Access: On-street parking. Three steps up from street, paved paths.
Things to see: The white-painted watch-house beside the gate has two windows but no chimney. Now used as a vestry.
Comments: A fine church with a Covenanters memorial in the kirkyard.

INCHINNAN

A mortsafe.

Address: Inchinnan Parish Church, Old Greenock Road, Inchinnan, PA4 9NJ.
NGR: NS47933 68912.
Lat, Long: 55.889251, -4.433048.
Access: Car park on site. Good paths.
Things to see: Mortsafes were in use here from 1818. The rental period was thirty days at 1s a day, with an additional fee of 5s for laying and removing. The collection of mortsafes has been transferred to St Conans in Argyll. One remains at the new church, in the glass-walled corridor.
Comments: The site of the old kirk, where the events occurred, lies under the runways of Glasgow Airport. The present church is starkly late twentieth-century.
Stories: 'Night after night, two men in turn from among the inhabitants watched the churchyard, gun or pistol in hand, from behind wall and tombstone, after every burial, till decay set in. Sometimes, it is said, the sound of a leaf or the cry of an animal, at the eerie, dread hour of midnight, put the watchers to flight, who, in their wild haste to escape, cast their weapons behind them; for superstition was then strong.' (*The Church & Parish of Inchinnan* by the Revd Robert McClelland.)

JOHNSTONE

A watch-house.

Address: Johnstone High Parish Church, Ludovic Square, Quarry Road, Johnstone, PA5 8EY.
NGR: NS42613 62966.
Lat, Long: 55.834179, -4.514571.
Access: Parking on site. Gravel paths.
Things to see: The watch-house at the entrance gates is in good condition.
Comments: The headstones in the extensive graveyard are all laid flat or set into the wall.

LOCHWINNOCH

An unusual watchtower.

Address: 'Auld Simon' Church, Johnshill, Lochwinnoch, PA12 4ER.
NGR: NS35592 59123.
Lat, Long: 55.797337, -4.624209.
Access: Parking in the village. Paved paths.
Things to see: When the old church was demolished in 1808 all that was left was a severely truncated crow-stepped gable with the bell-turret. The upper floor was then used as a watchtower, with windows inserted in the roof and rear wall, and a fireplace and chimney added.
Comments: This impressive curio is definitely worth a visit.

NEILSTON

A circular watch-house.

Address: Neilston Parish Church, Main Street, Neilston, G78 3DT.
NGR: NS48007 57347.
Lat, Long: 55.785454, -4.425393.
Access: Flat paved paths.
Things to see: Two 'Roundhouses' flank the gate. The one on the left was an offertory house, pressed into use as a watch-house. The other building is the Session House.
Comments: A fine and interesting church.

NEWTON MEARNS

Sentry boxes for watchmen.

Address: Mearns Parish Church, Mearns Road/Eaglesham Road, Newton Mearns, G77 5LZ.
NGR: NS543551.
Lat, Long: 55,766887, -4.324949.
Access: Large car park on site. The path from the gates slopes upward to the church on the mound.
Things to see: The gateposts take the form of sentry boxes, which must have been exceptionally dismal on a winter's night.
Comments: Excellent Georgian church with tall bell-tower.
Stories: Two men in a carriage were stopped at the Mearns toll-bar one night. When the toll-keeper waved his lantern in the face of their 'companion' on the seat between them, he commented on the man's appearance. They said that their friend was indeed very sick, which is why they were rushing him

The two 'sentry boxes' at Mearns Parish Church. The relief watchmen waited their turn in the warmer Session House to the left. *(Geoff Holder)*

home at this time of night. The unsuspecting keeper wished them happy trails, and in the early hours two relieved students delivered the corpse to College Street.

PAISLEY
Plentiful anecdotes.
In one of the most horrifying cases in the bodysnatching pantheon, seventeen-year-old surgeon's apprentice Alexander Taylor agreed to purchase what he thought was the corpse of Agnes Kelly's illegitimate baby. But when he met up in a Paisley garden with Matthew Smith, the child's father, he discovered the three-month-old girl was not dead – so Smith squeezed her throat and drowned her in a pond. The appalled (and probably terrified) Taylor took the murdered infant away and concealed the body, refusing to give any account of what had happened. Both Taylor and Smith were accused of abduction and murder, the former being acquitted on 2 February 1807 and the latter executed at Edinburgh on 11 March.

In 1824 the crew of a boat passing along Paisley Canal found the corpse of a girl below the water level, tied to a pier of Hawkhead bridge. The hands and feet had been bound and the 'package' was clearly intended for a pick-up from its hiding place.

In November 1828 a suspected snatcher was apprehended by an angry crowd in Abbey Street and taken to the police station, but the driver of the cart and horse parked suspiciously against the wall of the abbey graveyard was allowed to depart unmolested. On 8 December the cadaver of Helen Duncan was found missing from the burial-ground of the United Presbyterian Church on Oakshaw Street. The twenty-three-year-old had died of consumption and been buried four days previously. The snatchers had probably been disturbed, as the open grave was still exposed and the shroud in plain sight. Helen's father visited Glasgow without success, but that evening a young man in Back Sneddon Street said he had heard a strange noise at 3 a.m. in an unused garret close to his house. The room was searched and the body found tied up in a sack. The young woman's relatives conducted a re-interment the following day. Less than thirty minutes after the police left the premises, two strangers, muffled in cloaks, arrived at the garret and rummaged around. One was heard to exclaim, 'It is off, let us begone,' and both vanished into the night.

As elsewhere in Scotland, the Burke and Hare trial prompted the creation of a watching group. The Paisley Society for Protecting the Dead was formed in January 1829. Mortsafes were considered but rejected as too expensive due to the number required for the mortality rate of the populous city, so watching was the preferred option. At its height the Society had 7,000 members, paying 6d to join and 1d a quarter thereafter. A number of paid-up watchers were women. The Society purchased a number of wooden watch-boxes for the various churchyards, and provided them with grates, coals and firewood. The enthusiastic watching seems to have been generally effective. When the corpse of a young boy was suspected as having been taken, the Society had the grave opened to demonstrate that it had not been disturbed. In 1836, four years after the Anatomy Act, Paisley finally wound up its Society for Protecting the Dead, although the huts were still available to anyone who wished to watch a freshly-dug grave (but they would have to provide their own heating). Being wooden, the watchers' boxes have not survived.

The cholera epidemic of 1831 saw a great many deaths, especially among the working population. The situation in Paisley was desperate, and many in the medical profession worked tirelessly to care for the sick and limit the contagion. Despair and grief mixed with the pre-existing dislike of the medical profession fostered by the bodysnatching scandals, and soon a rumour spread that doctors were deliberately spreading the disease to obtain bodies for anatomical research, and that many coffins were buried empty. The reason given was that the graveyards were now so well watched that a new supply of corpses was required.

In this volatile atmosphere, some genuine resurrectionist work sparked a violent reaction. On 26 March two shovels and a rope with an iron hook were discovered at the Moss, a newly-constructed cholera burial-ground on the edge of town. The following day an excited crowd found an empty coffin. Wild rumours spread, and soon a large mob, armed with stakes and stones, marched into the city centre and system-atically attacked every doctor's dwelling and the Cholera Hospital on Oakshaw Street, then smashed the cholera van. Some looting also took place. Troops were called out, the Riot Act was read – which allowed the authorities to use severe force to control unrest – but confron-tation was avoided as the mob quickly dispersed. Special constables walked the streets through the night, but the fury of the violence was spent.

That night and the following day all the coffins in the cholera field were disinterred, and it was found that a total of three bodies had been taken, out of around eighty on the site. A seriously large reward of £50 was posted for the discovery of the resurrectionists, which seemed to calm matters, although no one was ever investigated. In May 1832, seven men pleaded guilty at the High Court of Justiciary in Glasgow to charges of mobbing and rioting. Sentences ranged from three to nine months in prison, remarkably lenient for the period. One man failed to appear at court and so was outlawed, while another pleaded not guilty and was committed for trial.

For Paisley, the consequences of the riot were severe: 420 panes of glass had been smashed, leading to a bill for the council of £104 7s 3d. Even worse, the medical men of the city universally resigned their positions as district surgeons and superintendents of the Cholera Hospital, and refused to care for any further cholera cases. In total, twenty-two doctors resigned in protest at their treatment by the mob.

RENFREW
Anecdote only.
Address: Renfrew Parish Church, 26 High Street, Renfrew, PA4 8TP.
NGR: NS50799 67547.
Lat, Long: 55.877904N, -4.386518W.
Access: Parking nearby. Level access.
Comments: A landmark spire.
Stories: A mortsafe was in use here from 1816, first being used on the grave of Mrs James Wilson. Supplied by Hume and Holms of Paisley, the charge was the same as at Inchinnan. On 10 February 1831 the body of Mrs Hugh Glen, the postmaster's wife, was stolen four weeks after the funeral. The grave had been left open and the dead-clothes scattered about; combined with the choice of the less-than-fresh subject, this suggests a team of snatchers notable for their ineptitude. The event caused a sensation, with crowds flocking to view the empty coffin.

🦇🦇🦇🦇🦇🦇🦇🦇🦇🦇🦇🦇🦇🦇🦇🦇

DUNBARTONSHIRE
BALDERNOCK
A good, small watch-house.
Address: Baldernock Parish Church, Craigmaddie Road, near Milngavie, East Dunbartonshire, G62 6HA (on the road from Strathblane to Bardowie, about a mile ENE of Milngavie).

NGR: NS57676 75062.

Lat, Long: 55.947386 -4.280294.

Access: Parking by entrance. Two steps at the gate. Paved paths on a slightly sloping site.

Things to see: A fine octagonal watch-house dated 1828.

Comments: An attractive country kirk.

BISHOPBRIGGS

Three different kinds of anti-bodysnatching devices in one place.

Address: Cadder Church, Cadder Road, Bishopbriggs, East Dunbartonshire, G64 3JJ.

NGR: NS61567 72319.

Lat, Long: 55.923963, -4.216989.

Access: Follow Cadder Road over the Forth and Clyde Canal, then narrow lane to right. Parking at the rear of the church. Churchyard is grassy and sloping.

Things to see: 1. Small freestanding watch-house with two window slits in each wall and one real and one dummy chimney. The door and front windows are grilled, allowing you to inspect the interior with its impressive fireplace. 2. A massive four-handled iron coffin, which took many men to lift. 3. A good example of a complete iron cage around a lair.

Comments: A substantial church in an excellent location atop a mound next to the canalside walkway. Definitely worth a visit.

CLACHAN OF CAMPSIE

A watch-house atop a mausoleum.

Address: St Machan's Church, Clachan Of Campsie, near Lennoxtown, East Dunbartonshire, G66 7AB.

NGR: NS61021 79641.

Lat, Long: 55.989542, -4.229496.

Access: Bus X5 from Buchanan Street Bus Station, Glasgow, or parking in adjacent square. Two steps up at gate. Interior of graveyard is grassy and uneven.

Things to see: When the bodysnatching scare took hold, a watch-house was raised on top of the Lennox family vault, a square mausoleum built in 1715. The resulting two-storeyed structure is now mouldering attractively, with a covering of ivy, an external

The watch-house at Cadder Church, Bishopbriggs. The iron coffin lies in the grass to the right. *(Geoff Holder)*

The watch-house above a mausoleum at Clachan of Campsie. The ground-floor doorway is composed of reused gravestones. *(Geoff Holder)*

stair to the upper floor, and a ground floor doorway composed of reused gravestones.

Comments: A beguiling country kirkyard ornamented with moss-covered tombstones and a fragmentary church ruin, set in a lovely hamlet popular with walkers.

Stories: Three men were on duty each night, with each householder having to take his turn. 'Scuffy', a local poacher and ne'er-do-well known to his mum as Robert Brown, made a point of keeping company at the watch-house, partly to help himself to the whisky, and partly so he could assess the degree of vigilance of the watch, and inform his bodysnatching comrades accordingly.

DUMBARTON
Anecdote only.

Address: Riverside Parish Church, High Street, Dumbarton, West Dunbartonshire, G82 1NB.

NGR: NS39729 75191.

Lat, Long: 55.942923N, 4.56717W.

Comments: A solid urban church with a fine spire. The graveyard and watch-house have been erased by urban development.

Stories: A slit in the watch-house wall allowed charitable citizens to donate coins into a collection box for the purchase of coal, firewood and warm clothes. A raid was foiled in 1829 but bodies were successfully lifted on two other occasions. In one case the rumour was that a deliberate deposit of herring scales, which reflected the lantern's glow in the dark, identified the targeted grave. Watching continued until 1836 or so.

KIRKINTILLOCH
A unique watchtower above an arch.

Address: Auld Aisle Cemetery, Old Aisle Road, Oxgangs, Kirkintilloch, East Dunbartonshire, G66 3HH.

NGR: NS66503 73105.

Lat, Long: 55.932416, -4.138447.

Access: Parking on-site next to the arch. The old graveyard (through the arch) is wooded and overgrown, making wheelchair access impossible.

Things to see: 1. The eighteenth-century arch was built as an entrance to the graveyard using the stones of the now-vanished medieval parish church. It is topped by a small square watch-house, reached by an external stair and surmounted by a bellcote which housed the mort bell that tolled at funerals. The bell may also have been rung if the watchmen needed assistance. 2. Three caged lairs.

Comments: Adjacent is the town's main cemetery, established in 1863.

Stories: In February 1831 a young girl saw a sack thrown over the cemetery wall, and raised the alarm. The three snatchers escaped, but left behind their prize, the body of a recently-buried old woman. The raid was remarkable for having taken place in broad daylight.

❦ ❦ ❦ ❦ ❦ ❦ ❦ ❦ ❦ ❦ ❦ ❦ ❦ ❦ ❦ ❦

SOUTH LANARKSHIRE
CARLUKE
Anecdote only.

On 11 January 1831, a carriage known as a 'Noddy' was spotted driving south through Wishaw. Everyone knew it must have been carrying bodysnatchers, as it was a fancy big-city vehicle almost unknown in this area. The citizens of Wishaw reacted by throwing up a barricade to block the inevitable return journey to Glasgow. That night the carriage was stopped and searched twice, traces of earth on the floor indicating that the travellers had been warned of the ambuscade and had dumped the body. The two men were held until morning, when a large crowd accompanied them along the road to Carluke. About a mile outside Wishaw a shallow grave was uncovered, containing the corpse of Elizabeth Hamilton, a middle-aged resident of Carluke who had been buried on 30 December.

The action now moved to the Crown Inn in Carluke, where the two men were besieged by the growing mob. In a repeat of the episode with William Hare at Dumfries, the Noddy was brought to the front of the inn as if the prisoners were about to leave on it. As the crowd vented its fury on the carriage (and someone cannily stole the valuable horse), the resurrectionists, accompanied by the Procurator-Fiscal and a troop of mounted soldiers, snuck out the back and galloped to Lanark Jail. The men were identified as Peter Craig and Glasgow surgeon John Stevenson, while their local contact – who had passed on the information about the body, and then warned them about the barricade – was named as William Ritchie, a stonemason from Carluke. As all three had participated in the lifting, they were charged collectively, but there is no record of a trial having taken place.

CRAWFORDJOHN
A watch-house in poor condition.
Address: Crawfordjohn Museum, Main Street, Crawfordjohn, ML12 6SS (three miles west of Abington).
NGR: NS88019 23823.
Lat, Long: 55.495321, -3.774073.
Access: Parking at the museum. Gravel paths.
Things to see: The rectangular watch-house still has its door, window and chimney, but the roof is dodgy.
Comments: The church is now the rural life museum of the Crawfordjohn Heritage Venture, open 2 p.m. to 5 p.m. Saturday and Sunday, from May until the end of September.

EAST KILBRIDE
From watch-house to public house.
Address: East Kilbride Parish Church, junction of Hunter Street and Montgomery Street, The Village, East Kilbride, G74 4LT.
NGR: NS63555 54526.
Lat, Long: 55.764768, -4.176246.
Access: Via the cobbled square in front of the pub.
Things to see: The watch-house at the churchyard entrance, built in 1827, is now part of the adjacent Montgomerie Arms.
Comments: The village is the older part of East Kilbride, predating the new town.

HAMILTON
A simple watch-house.
Address: Hamilton Old Parish Church, Cadzow Lane, Hamilton, ML3 6AY.
NGR: NS72350 55571.
Lat, Long: 55.776562, -4.036655.
Access: Parking on the nearby streets. Level access through ornate gates onto gravel paths.
Things to see: The watch-house next to the gate is basically just a large sentry box, with a flat roof and a simple pediment over the door. It now stores the refuse bins and wheelbarrows.
Comments: A striking Georgian church, designed by William Adam.
Stories: Some men out walking with their dogs on a Sunday in March 1823 discovered the cadaver of sixty-year-old Susan Sellie, tied up into a small bundle and hidden in the bushes. Two other empty graves were found. Presumably the snatchers had intended to return for this third corpse – or had they abandoned it because they had reached their carrying limit?

LANARK
Anecdote only.
Address: Old St Kentigern's Churchyard, Hyndford Road, Lanark, ML11 9AU.
NGR: NS88026 43812.
Lat, Long: 55.669499, -3.768334.
Access: Tarmac paths and well-kept grass.
Comments: The remains of the medieval kirkyard, and some good stones.
Stories: In January 1821, weaver William Crawfurd (buried at the end of the previous month) and middle-aged Janet Brown of New Lanark (buried 13 January) were both lifted. A week later the enraged inhabitants of Lanark learned of the drama that had played out on the road to Edinburgh, at Kirknewton. Some labourers there had become suspicious of a group that they had seen passing the previous day on the way towards Lanark. The single horse was in a bad state (as it turned out it had been hitched to the cart for more than thirty hours continuously, and had pulled five men for over fifty miles on its journey from and

towards Edinburgh – the poor creature must have been on its last legs). The labourers ran to the tollhouse to give the alarm, and when the cart was stopped an awful smell issued from its cargo. The driver threatened the angry crowd with his whip, but the customs officer used his authority to order the packages opened.

Of the five men, two were quickly released for lack of evidence (they had been walking some distance behind the cart, and stated that they had nothing to do with the other three, whom they'd 'never seen before'). John Kerr was released because his case was inconclusive, while Andrew Miller and Thomas Hodge were arrested and a near-riot ensued when they arrived in Lanark. They received twelve months' imprisonment apiece. Once he got out of jail, Hodge was quickly in trouble again, this time at Larbert (see the Falkirk chapter).

STRATHAVEN

A truly unique anti-bodysnatching head.
Address: John Hastie Museum, Threestanes Road, Strathaven, ML10 6DX. **NGR**: NS699 447.
Lat, Long: 55.678737, -4.070532.
Access: Open 12 p.m. to 4.30 p.m. on Friday, Saturday and Sunday between April and September. Admission free. Wheelchair ramp available on request.
Things to see: Possibly the most bizarre anti-bodysnatching item in this book is the 'guardian head', a carved stone figure dating from the 1820s.
Comments: This small local history collection covers agriculture, industry and the 'Killing Times' of the Covenanting period. Look out for the jar of pickled snakes.

SYMINGTON

A diminutive watch-house.
Address: Parish Church, Kirk Bauk, Symington, ML12 6LA (west of Biggar).
NGR: NS99869 35132.
Lat, Long: 55.59974, -3.590682.
Access: Parking outside. Level access via beaten earth paths.

Things to see: The tiny watch-house beside the gate has two slit windows, and steps up to the door.
Comments: A pleasant wee church.

🙶🙶🙶🙶🙶🙶🙶🙶🙶🙶🙶🙶🙶🙶🙶🙶

NORTH LANARKSHIRE

KILSYTH

An impressive watchtower.
Address: Howe Road Burial-ground, Kilsyth, G65 0LP.
NGR: NS71710 77238.
Lat, Long: 55.970944, -4.057129.
Access: A grassy and sloping site.
Things to see: The solid octagonal watchtower has a flight of stone steps leading up to the first floor, where peeking through the iron yett gives a view of the watcher's fireplace and graveyard-commanding Gothic-arched windows. The gate on the ground floor is for the mausoleum of Jean Cochrane

The John Hastie Museum: 'This head was placed each night in the window of a cottage beside the graveyard gates, back-lit with a candle. This was to give the impression that a vigilant lookout was on duty.' *(South Lanarkshire Museums)*

and her son, whose deaths are recorded in an extensive inscription on one wall.

Comments: The tower has recently been beautifully restored.

🙊 🙊 🙊 🙊 🙊 🙊 🙊 🙊 🙊 🙊 🙊 🙊 🙊 🙊 🙊 🙊

AYRSHIRE

AYR

A mortsafe in an atmospheric city graveyard.

Address: Auld Kirk of Ayr, Blackfriars Walk, Ayr, South Ayrshire, KA7 1TT.

NGR: NS33900 21920.

Lat, Long: 55.462877, -4.628696.

Access: Along the cobbled Kirk Port off High Street, or from the Blackfriars Walk riverside path.

Things to see: Two parts of a frame-shaped mortsafe attached to the inner walls of the lychgate at Kirk Port.

Comments: An extensive graveyard open to the riverfront, with many interesting memorials. Some vandalism.

Stories: In autumn 1829 two boxes arrived by boat from Stranraer, with an onward address to Glasgow. The smell gave away the contents, and three bodies were discovered. They had presumably been transshipped from Ireland. Shortly afterwards, a late-night drinking party heard a carriage arrive at the building where the bodies had been temporarily deposited. While his companions raised the alarm, one man removed the wheel screws, so that when the carriage left it swiftly lost its wheels.

The crowd took the bodies and assaulted the driver, who somehow repaired his vehicle and fled for his life. At Kilmarnock a group of miners, forewarned by a mail driver, annihilated the carriage with a volley of stones. The local people had secretly buried the bodies by the shore, and when the authorities attempted to recover them, a party dug them up, took a boat, and buried them at sea.

ALLOWAY

A mortsafe in the heart of Burns Country.

Address: Alloway Auld Kirk, Alloway Street, Ayr, South Ayrshire, KA7 4PQ.

NGR: NS33191 18051.

Lat, Long: 55.427874, -4.637598.

Access: Parking at the Tam O'Shanter Experience along the road opposite. Several steps up from street level.

Things to see: Two parts of a frame-shaped mortsafe stand in a locked part of the roofless church; they can be easily viewed through the gates.

Comments: A small churchyard much visited because it holds the grave of the father of Robert Burns. Fans of the poet will find many other Burns-related attractions in the immediate area.

FENWICK

Two sentry boxes and a morthouse in a lovely setting.

Address: Parish Church, Kirkton Road, Fenwick, East Ayrshire, KA3 6DJ.

One half of the mortsafe at Auld Kirk of Ayr. *(Geoff Holder)*

The two parts of the mortsafe at Alloway Old Kirk. *(Geoff Holder)*

NGR: NS46478 43479.
Lat, Long: 55.660492, -4.441966.
Access: Car park behind church. Easy access and good paths.
Things to see: 1. A pair of sentry boxes dated 1828, one at each gate. The six-sided structures have no fireplace or windows, which meant that watchers would have needed to keep the door open at all times – they must have been dismal places to spend the night. 2. A ruinous morthouse or caged lair stands in one corner, its solid walls topped by a framework of iron bars.
Comments: A delightful churchyard holding several Covenanters' graves.

Each gate at Fenwick Church has a sentry box.
(Geoff Holder)

IRVINE

The gravestones of two local bodysnatchers.
Address: Irvine Old Parish Church, Kirkgate, Irvine, North Ayrshire, KA12 0DD.
NGR: NS32177 38638.
Lat, Long: 55.612311, -4.666076.
Access: Parking directly in front of the church. The church is on a slight hill but the paths are good.
Things to see: The gravestones of resurrectionists John Fletcher and James Wilson. Both are west of the church, a few yards from the front door, Fletcher's being a recumbent stone with a faded inscription, lying south of the central path, while Wilson's is north of the path, supported by metal props.
Comments: An extensive graveyard with many well-carved stones, surrounding a striking church. Some vandalism.
Stories: In 1826 the discovery of an empty grave led to the revelation that another eleven had also been rifled. The chief suspects were Robert Stein (a Glasgow carter with local connections), William Anderson (butcher), James Wilson (sexton), and John Fletcher, the brilliant young town doctor. Nothing was ever proved, but Fletcher was finished socially in Irvine, and moved to Ayr, where he died four years later.

KILMARNOCK

Anecdote only.
Address: Laigh Kirk, John Dickie Street, Kilmarnock, East Ayrshire, KA1 1HA.
NGR: NS42767 37948.
Lat, Long: 55.609655, -4.497731.
Access: Easy access next to the kirk.
Stories: Robert Laurie planned to be buried alongside his father. The only problem was that his father lay in Laigh churchyard, while Robert's lair was in another kirkyard (possibly Riccarton). So, one winter's night the veteran of Waterloo dug up his father's remains and carried them away for burial at the other site – but not before Robert popped into a pub for a drink or three, placing the bag of bones beside his glass.

KIRKMICHAEL

Anecdote only.
Address: Kirkmichael Church, Patna Road, Kirkmichael, South Ayrshire, KA19 7NU.
NGR: NS34543 08981.
Lat, Long: 55.346919, -4.610884.
Access: Level access through the lychgate. Parking in the village.
Comments: A lovely graveyard with a number of good carved stones.

Stories: In March 1829 the discovery of an empty grave prompted a mass exhumation, leading to between twenty-one and twenty-three coffins being found empty. The burials had taken place over the previous six months. The *Glasgow Herald* for 9 March 1829 described the scene: 'The empty coffins are brought up, and the dead clothes, fresh and white, exhibited across the graves; the relatives are rushing from every part of the parish to know the fate of their departed friends, and it is not easy to describe the anguish they feel when their removal is discovered. The perpetrators have, in some instances, left the bodies of such as have not suited their purpose in a situation too shocking to describe.' The gravedigger promptly vanished, with a reward for his arrest on his heels.

Auchenharvie Castle near Torryburn. It has been a ruin since the eighteenth century. *(Author's Collection)*

MAYBOLE

Anecdote only.

A carter named Morrow was often suspected of transporting bodies along with his usual cargo, a notion apparently confirmed when in 1832 a drunk man named McLelland fell asleep on Morrow's cart and woke up next to a corpse. Unfortunately, by the time the police arrived, Morrow was on his way to Ayr and when they searched the cart there was no body to be seen – everyone suspected it had been dumped at the doctor's house on Redbrae. The carter was thereafter known as 'Burke' Morrow, and lived with the reputation as a resurrectionist for many years.

SORN

Anecdote only.

Address: Parish Church, Main Street, Sorn (near Catrine), East Ayrshire, KA5 6HT.
NGR: NS55021 26754.
Lat, Long: 55.512960, -4.297500.
Access: Parking in the village, easy access.
Comments: Simple church with several interesting gravestones.
Stories: In February 1824 a distraught father travelled to Glasgow, where he traced and confronted the men who had recently lifted his daughter. They agreed to restore the body on the condition that he did not prosecute them,

and he found the 'package' in a house in the Gallowgate. The authorities then stepped in and issued three warrants for Glasgow medical students, who promptly left the country.

TORRYBURN

Temporary storage for corpses in a castle.

Address: Auchenharvie Castle, Auchenharvie Farm, on minor road north-east of Torranyard (off A736), East Ayrshire, KA13 7RB.
NGR: NS36281 44310.
Lat, Long: 55.664621, -4.604372.
Access: Exterior viewing only.
Things to see: A much-ruined medieval tower.
Comments: The site is unstable and dangerous.
Stories: The castle was allegedly where resurrectionists deposited their merchandise overnight, for collection by cart the following day. Daytime travellers would not cause any suspicion when stopped at the toll-bars.

TROON

Anecdote only.

The toll-keeper at Loans Toll near Troon took pity on two travellers in the cold weather and let them warm themselves by his fire. He took a glass of whisky out to the driver of a gig, and, on getting no response, found the 'man' was in fact a corpse wrapped in a coat.

SOUTHERN SCOTLAND

> 'Oh, father, I should so like to be a Resurrection-Man when I'm quite growed up!'
>
> Charles Dickens, *A Tale of Two Cities*

THE BORDERS

ANCRUM

Anecdote only.

Address: Old Ancrum Church, Ancrum, Roxburghshire, TD8 6UJ.

NGR: NT62150 24885.

Lat, Long: 55.515770, -2.600399.

Access: On a cul-de-sac north off the B6400 just west of the village. Access is via a field gate into an avenue; well-kept grass.

Comments: An attractive ivy-covered ruined church. Its replacement was erected in the late nineteenth century.

Stories: In 1825 a decomposed female corpse was found partially hidden in a nearby quarry. The body had been made into a package the size of an average hand-carried bundle – the arms were tightly bound to the body with the hands on the shoulders, and the legs similarly corded, bent backwards to the thighs. Another rope went from the knee joints to the neck. It had then been sewn into a small sack and sealed with string and wax. The cadaver was taken to Ancrum Church where some time later it was identified by a man from Bedrule – his daughter's grave had been violated a few weeks previously. The mystery of why the corpse was left uncollected was solved when the culprits turned out to be a pair in jail in Jedburgh. They had been apprehended while raiding graves there and had been in custody for the past fortnight.

CHANNELKIRK

Anecdote only.

Address: Parish Church, Channelkirk House, Kirktonhill, Berwickshire, TD2 6PT (on a minor road north of Oxton).

NGR: NT48149 54505.

Lat, Long: 55.780928, -2.815743.

Access: A slightly sloping grassy spot.

Comments: The church is a striking pink; a lovely quiet spot.

Stories: A farmer named Hogg, working by the road ascending Soutra Fell, found the bodies of two children hidden in a conduit beneath a low bridge over a ravine. An armed party waited to ambush the returning resurrectionists but they gave themselves away and the one-horse trap rushed past without stopping. The tunnel was thereafter named the 'Bairnies' Conduit'. As a result of this episode a mortsafe was deployed. This did not prevent another theft, that of a stout woman who lived at The Dass (a byre at Nether Howden Farm).

CHIRNSIDE

A watch-house.

Address: Parish Church, Kirkgate, Chirnside, Berwickshire, TD11 3XL.

NGR: NT86960 56020.

Lat, Long: 55.797294, -2.209558.

Access: Level paved access through a monumental archway.

Things to see: The red sandstone watch-house is a tad underwhelming, being a small structure with a single-pitched roof and a blocked window.

Comments: A very attractive church in a nice setting.

COLDINGHAM

A possible morthouse or watch-house?

Address: Coldingham Priory Church, High Street, Coldingham, Berwickshire, TD14 5NE.

NGR: NT90358 65969.

Lat, Long: 55.886765, -2.155718.

Access: Car park adjacent. A well-kept level site.

Things to see: The small building by the car park entrance may have been a morthouse. The watch-house appears to have disappeared – or was it the same building?

Comments: The imposing church is on the site of the medieval priory, some evocative traces of which still survive.

Stories: According to the Coldingham village website, a body hidden in a trunk was discovered on its way out of the village in 1820. The local physician, Dr Lawrie, was imprisoned for six months at Greenlaw, then for a further six weeks at the Canongate Tollbooth in Edinburgh.

COLDSTREAM/LENNEL

A morthouse and a mortstone.

Address: Lennel Old Parish Church, Lennel, Coldstream, Berwickshire, TD12 4EU (north-east of the village on the A6112).

NGR: NT85740 41173.

Lat, Long: 55.663859, -2.228237.

Access: Rough grass, on a mound, and somewhat overgrown.

Things to see: 1. The stone-walled shed with the corrugated-iron roof inside the west end of the ruined church was built in 1821 as a morthouse. 2. A coffin-shaped mortstone lies embedded in the grass north of the ruin, with the impression where the metal band kept it in place clearly visible; there is allegedly a second example somewhere nearby.

Comments: A splendid and atmospheric site. Interpretation panel.

Stories: There used to be a sign here reading: 'Take notice. An armed watch is placed here every night for the protection of this burial-ground. And has orders to fire upon any person who may enter at improper hours without permission.'

ECKFORD

A petite watchtower.

Address: Parish Church, Kirkbank, Eckford,

Roxburghshire, TD5 8LN (north of the village on the A698).

NGR: NT70619 27058.

Lat, Long: 55.530084, -2.473342.

Access: The site is on a grassy mound with gravel paths.

Things to see: A bijou cylindrical watchtower with crenellated parapet, slit windows and steps up to the wrought-iron gate covering the door. Sadly the old flintlock musket used by the watchers has disappeared.

Comments: A set of punishment jougs hang on the church wall.

Stories: In 1829 James Goodfellow, a young packman from Kelso also known as Dandy Jim, was returning from a late-night assignation with his sweetheart when he saw a faint light in the churchyard, followed by the unmistakable sound of men digging. Bumping into a horse and gig, mischief entered his mind. The horse was sent galloping off across country, with the resurrectionists in hot pursuit, allowing Jim to hide the corpse and take its place in its travelling wrap. On a lonely part of the road near the village of Maxwellheugh, one of the bodysnatchers – who were a pair of tailors from Greenlaw – leaned against the 'cadaver' and exclaimed, 'The corpse is warm!' At this point Jim sat up, lifted the cloth from his face, and spoke in deep sepulchral tones: 'Warm, do you say? And pray, what would you be if ye came frae where I ha'e been?' Both miscreants leapt from the gig, which Dandy Jim then happily drove to Kelso; no-one claimed either vehicle or beast, so he became their possessor by default, and made a tidy profit thereby.

The eagle-eyed will spot that this is yet another variation on the 'substituted corpse that comes alive' urban legend, and is almost identical to the story told at Kirkhill in Highland Region.

EDROM

Anecdote only.

Address: Parish Church, Edrom, Berwickshire, TD11 3PX.

NGR: NT82760 55835.

Lat, Long: 55.795633, -2.276696.

Access: Signposted from the village. Car park on site. Gravel paths.

Comments: The site is in the care of Historic Scotland, on account of the richly carved Romanesque doorway of the former church.

Stories: In 1825 (or 1828) a farmer (or a farmer with his innkeeper friend) came across two men riding in a gig with a suspiciously unmoving third figure between them. A chase commenced on the moonlit roads, with the two snatchers eventually abandoning their vehicle and running off into the darkness. When the gig was taken to Duns the corpse was found to belong to a Mr MacGall, just buried at Edrom. Due to the strength of feeling in the town, the body was reburied in Duns, while the carriage was dragged into the market square and burned by an angry mob.

EYNMOUTH

A unique watch-house – but is it what it seems?

Address: Old Cemetery, High Street, Eynmouth, Berwickshire, TD14 5EW.

NGR: NT94340 64425.

Lat, Long: 55.872954, -2.092025.

Access: Steps up from High Street or Albert Road. Car park opposite.

Things to see: To the right as you enter, a strange watch-house lurks in the bushes, its walls composed of gravestones carved with skulls, bones and other symbols of mortality. Things, however, are not what they seem. In 1849 the cemetery became overfilled following a cholera epidemic, and so 6ft of earth was added to re-level the space. The horizontal gravestones were simply covered over, while the vertical ones were re-used in the retaining wall. As part of the operations, a watch-house on the other side of the entrance was swept away. By 1849, of course, the resurrectionist scare was long past; nevertheless this new watch-house was built. Traditions changed slowly in the Borders even when the need for them had passed, but given the date and the fact that only the best-carved tombstones were used, I suggest the present bizarre structure may be nothing more than an antiquarian folly.

Comments: Navigate by the memorial with the broken mast, as there are no gravestones.

GORDON

An overgrown watch-house.

Address: St Michael's Kirk, Manse Road, Gordon, Berwickshire, TD3 6LS.

NGR: NT64490 43188.

Lat, Long: 55.680887, -2.566318.

Access: Eight steps at the entrance; gravel paths.

Things to see: The ivy-strewn watch-house has a pitched roof, although further details are hard to make out.

Comments: The church of 1897 replaced earlier models.

HOBKIRK

Graverobbing a ghostbuster.

Address: Hobkirk Church, Hobkirk, Roxburghshire, TD9 8JU (on minor road just south of Bonchester Bridge).

NGR: NT58722 10895.

Lat, Long: 55.391374, -2.656070.

Access: Park on the verge. Gravel path, well-tended grass.

Comments: A nice quiet country spot, with a fine church.

Stories: In 1720 the Revd Nicol Edgar laid to rest a murdered cattle dealer whose ghost had taken to haunting Hobkirk churchyard. Far from giving thanks for rescuing them from the frightening phantom, the ungrateful villagers came to regard the ghostbusting minister as 'uncanny', even cursed. When he died four years later, the consensus was that his spirit would wander. So it was decided to cast his body into the wilderness. What happened next was recorded in *North and South of Tweed* by Jean Lang:

> The resurrectionists broke open the coffin, tied a rope tightly round the body of their dead minister, binding his arms close to his sides, and swung off with their burden towards Bonchester Hill.

They were half-way to the spot they had fixed upon when, in crossing a deep syke, one of the bearers stumbled and roughly jerked the corpse. One of the arms got loose from the rope, and the chill dead hand of the minister violently smote the face of one of his bearers. It was more than enough to cause a panic amongst those who had already fancied that they saw strange forms and heard dread noises, and whose hearts had grown chilled by the stillness and loneliness of the dark June night. The body was dropped without ceremony amongst the bracken in the syke, and the resurrectionists fancied all the warlocks, ghosts, and evil things of the nether world in pursuit as they ran, at heart-bursting speed, back to their homes at Hobkirk.

The following evening a different party returned the body to its rightful grave.

KIRKURD
A fine watch-house.
Address: Kirkurd Old Parish Church, Kirkurd, Peeblesshire, EH46 7AH (south of Blyth Bridge on the A701).
NGR: NT12770 44274.
Lat, Long: 55.684065, -3.388919.
Access: Parking outside. Gravel paths.
Things to see: The very obvious watch-house (dated 1828) has boarded-up windows on three sides and a tall chimney.
Comments: The church has been deconsecrated and is used as a store.

LAUDER
A possible watch-house above a hearse garage.
Address: Old Parish Church, Market Place, Lauder, Berwickshire, TD2 6TB.
NGR: NT53095 47541.
Lat, Long: 55.718999, -2.748236.
Access: Easy access to a mostly grassed site.
Things to see: The vestry and hearse-house (now used as a church centre) facing onto Mid Row has windows overlooking the graveyard and probably also served also as a watch-house. A separate morthouse (or was it a second watch-house?) has vanished.
Comments: An imposing church in the centre of the village.
Stories: The morthouse/watch-house was built in 1830, following a bodysnatching raid.

OXNAM
A small watch-house.
Address: Parish Church, Oxnam, Roxburghshire, TD8 6RD (north of the village on a minor road past the manse).
NGR: NT70118 18998.
Lat, Long: 55.463337, -2.473902.
Access: Tarmac paths and level access.
Things to see: The small watch-house in the south-east corner is in good condition, although the window has been blocked-up.
Comments: A plain church with a set of punishment jougs on one wall.

PEEBLES
A watchtower.
Address: St Andrew's Church and Cemetery, Neidpath Road, Peebles, Peebles-shire, EH45 8JQ.
NGR: NT24592 40646.
Lat, Long: 55.653468, -3.199943.
Access: Parking on site. Paved paths in a well cared-for cemetery.
Things to see: The tall Victorianised tower, all that remains of the medieval church, was used as a watch-house.
Comments: The old graveyard melds into the modern cemetery.
Stories: Two strangers casually made enquiries in the Tontine Hotel (still there on High Street) about the parish minister's residence, and made great pretence of going to see him. But, on their trips to and from the inn, they actually lifted a body, and got it past the Edinburgh road toll-keeper by dressing it in a cloak and hat. Episodes such as this prompted the creation of a watching society. One night James Brydon, shoemaker Robert Brydon and weaver Charles Spottiswoode were on duty when a raiding party was spotted. Brydon fired his weapon,

The old steeple of St Andrew's Church in Peebles, used as a watchtower. *(Leslie Thomson)*

and although the snatchers escaped, blood was found on the rail around the grave, and on the kirkyard wall. Elijah Henderson, who lived at Hay Lodge, ran out in his night-shirt brandishing a pitchfork; it seems the watchers thought he was a white-shrouded ghost, an impression only dispelled when he spoke to them. The raid was blamed, possibly without justification, on a visiting teacher of chemistry, who was forced to abandon his lectures in the town. Tweeddale Museum on the High Street has a watcher's gun and chair from Linton church, which can be viewed on request.

SANQUHAR
Anecdotes only.

If the following story is true, it demonstrates that some bodysnatchers deliberately, or carelessly, entertained a high degree of risk. One summer day, just after midday, a gig with a lady and gentleman came into the town from the west and paused at the inn at the Townfoot, where the man dismounted and took a glass of whisky. Some weavers were at their post-mealtime leisure and started to inspect the fine quality of the carriage and horse. But there was something odd about the lady – she sat stiffly, heavily veiled and cloaked, making not the slightest movement… By the time the penny dropped, the man was back at the reins, and urged the horse through the gathering crowd, whipping one man who tried to take the bridle. Who the resurrection man was, and from where he had stolen the corpse, remained a mystery.

Certainly the area around the town was subject to depredations. Medical student John Thomson, the son of Dr Thomson of Sanquhar, turned up for his dissecting class in Edinburgh to find his subject was a man he knew, an old blind fiddler who had been buried in Sanquhar kirkyard only a few days previously.

TRAQUAIR
Anecdote only.

Address: Parish Church, Kirkhouse, Traquair, Peebles-shire, EH44 6PU (one mile south of Traquair).
NGR: NT32006 33465.
Lat, Long: 55.590047, -3.080367.
Access: Parking near the gate. Gravel paths on a slightly sloping site.
Comments: A lonely spot, beautiful in the right weather.
Stories: The Traquair Churchyard Waiting Society (later called Traquair Watch House Society) commenced in 1824 with seventy-three Ordinary members aged between sixteen and sixty. Youths paid 1s 6d entry fee, while older men coughed up 2s 6d. Honorary members, (that is to say, the big landowners) paid £1 1s, and Extraordinary members were charged £1, but were not required to watch in person as long as they could provide a substitute such as a servant; a fine of 2s was

levied for each failure to do so. Inevitably the bulk of the watching duties fell on the Ordinary members, who worked on a rota or put up a substitute (failure to appear in person or in proxy attracted a substantial fine of 5s). In 1832 the graveyard was watched for 329 consecutive nights – forty-seven weeks of nightly labour, an incredible burden for such a small community. Two guns were purchased for £1 10s. The first accommodation was an unsatisfactory temporary hut, so the watchers were given use of a nearby building. By the 1870s the watch-house was being used as a shelter for homeless people, much to the displeasure of the uppercrust neighbours. The watch-house has now gone.

WHITSOME
A fine watch-house.
Address: Old Parish Churchyard, Whitsome, TD11 3NA Berwickshire, (south-west of Duns on the B6437).
NGR: NT86224 50349.
Lat, Long: 55.746309, -2.221016.
Access: Park at the modern cemetery then walk 300 yards along a green lane to the old graveyard. The grassed site is on a slight rise.
Things to see: The 1820 overgrown watch-house stands on the summit of the mound, the windows blocked-up and the chimney gone. However, the door is missing so you can poke around inside.
Comments: The church has vanished.

DUMFRIES & GALLOWAY
DUMFRIES
Watchers' sentry boxes and the last sighting of William Hare.
Address: St Michael Church, St Michael Street, Dumfries DG1 2PY.
NGR: NX97552 75692.
Lat, Long: 55.065158, -3.606308.
Access: Car park at rear of the church, off Wallace Street. Flight of steps at the entrance.
Things to see: The main entrance gates are flanked by massive white-painted dual-function gateposts/sentry boxes, each topped by a classical urn. These were probably used by watchers, although they would have been uncomfortable and miserable refuges. The other possibility is that they were designed for some ceremonial function, perhaps connected with events around the white-domed mausoleum that marks the burial place of Robert Burns.
Comments: This city church has an impressive spire and several elaborately-carved tombstones in the extensive graveyard.
Stories: On the night of 5 February 1829 William Hare, serial killer, the Crown's star witness against his partner Burke, and a free man given immunity from the law, was put on a coach under the assumed name of Mr Black. The intention was for him to slip off to Ireland unnoticed. But at Noblehouse, twenty miles south of Edinburgh, Hare was recognised by a passenger. By the time the coach arrived at Dumfries, everyone knew one of the Westport murderers was in their midst. An angry mob, many thousands strong, laid siege to the King's Arms Hotel in the High Street, where Hare was lodged while waiting for his coach to Portpatrick. Some enraged citizens managed to force their way inside intent on killing him, but he was secured in an upstairs room for safety.

The rest of the day saw the authorities play a cat-and-mouse game with the potentially violent crowd. The Portpatrick coach left at 11 a.m. It was forcibly stopped and searched, but Hare was not on it. At 3 p.m. a two-horse chaise was brought to the front of the hotel and ostentatiously loaded with a travelling trunk. It then set off with the mob in hot pursuit while Hare was unceremoniously ejected through a rear window and taken by another carriage to the tollbooth in Buccleuch Street. The enraged mob attacked the prison doors and smashed windows and lamps, so 100 special constables were quickly sworn in and armed with batons to support the local militia. By 1 a.m. the near-riot was over, the crowd dispersed into the chilly night, and Hare was covertly escorted out of town. The Portpatrick road was watched and Galloway was forewarned of his coming, so it was decided to take him along the road to Annan and England. Left to his own devices after a few miles, he was seen twice near Carlisle in the next few days. He then vanishes from the official record.

Rumour had it that in later years a well-known blind beggar in London was secretly Hare, having lost his eyes to a quicklime attack. He was also supposedly lynched in Londonderry and executed at New York – alleged sightings of Hare were legion, as he became Georgian Britain's equivalent of Elvis. In all probability he simply returned to Ireland and contrived to live in anonymity. Some weeks after the Dumfries incident a woman arrived at the King's Arms (which is now Boots the Chemist), claiming to be Hare's sister, saying he had asked her to retrieve his bundle of clothes that had been left behind in the confusion. They were still lying, untouched, in a corner of the top room where he had been sequestered.

DUMFRIES MUSEUM
A fine mortsafe.
Address: Church Street, Dumfries, DG2 7SW.
NGR: NX975 758.
Lat, Long: 55.066466, -3.606101.
Access: Open April to September, Monday to Saturday 10 a.m. to 5 p.m., October to March, Tuesday to Saturday 10 a.m. to 1 p.m. and 2 p.m. to 5 p.m. Admission free. There is a lift to the first floor where the mortsafe resides.
Things to see: The mortsafe appears to be of the type purchased for personal use by families of means – a relatively light construction of two diagonal bars joining into a single spine supporting four 'cages' to hold the coffin. They were typically buried permanently with the coffin, unlike the more robust and heavier examples which were usually purchased by the parish and rented out for each new burial. The mortsafe is not displayed to the best advantage, and better views can be found on the Future Museum website, http://future-museum.co.uk.
Comments: A fine museum in a former windmill.

TUNDERGARTH
A watch-house converted to a memorial to the Lockerbie disaster.
Address: Parish Church, Tundergarth, DG11 2PU (On B7068 east of Lockerbie).
NGR: NY17476 80748.
Lat, Long: 55.114608, -3.294868.
Access: Good tarmac paths.
Things to see: The plain rectangular watch-house has been converted into a memorial room for the victims of the Lockerbie Air Disaster, murdered by a terrorist bomb on 21 December 1988. The Book of Remembrance can be consulted.
Comments: Good carved gravestones and the roofless ivy-clad ruin of the former church.

THE FORTH VALLEY

'A body-snatcher!' whispered Beck, with a shudder … 'He lives with graves, and churchyards, and stiff 'uns.'

Lord Lytton, *Lucretia*

FALKIRK

AIRTH

A trio of excellent iron coffins.
Address: Old Parish Church, Airth, FK2 8JF (next to Airth Castle Hotel).
NGR: NS90034 86876.
Lat, Long: 56.062046, -3.767650.
Access: Park at the hotel. Reasonably level access.
Things to see: The abandoned graveyard rejoices in three massive iron coffins, inscribed with the word 'Airth' followed by a date – 1831, 1832 and 1837. The one by the tower may be hard to see but the pair beside the wall can be fully inspected.
Comments: Part of the site is unsafe.

AIRTH – CLUB'S TOMB

One man's attempt to foil the resurrectionists.
Address: Club's Tomb, FK2 8RU (between Westfield and Powbridge on the B9124 west of Airth).
NGR: NS88129 87460.
Lat, Long: 56.065148, -3.797991.
Access: The building is in a field on the south side of the road.
Things to see: Buried beneath the vegetation is a stout-walled mausoleum with the door missing, thus allowing access to the rubbish-filled vault. The roof, now virtually invisible, was once pyramidal.
Comments: A real oddity.
Stories: The mausoleum was built by farmer James Club of Westfield, whose Will, registered 29 July 1757, stated that he wished to be buried in the vault, along with his dog, beyond the reach of the resurrectionists. This is a remarkably early date for such precautions.

BO'NESS

Anecdote only.
Each householder had to take his turn at watching or find a substitute; some local men virtually made a profession out of it, as watchers were paid 1s a night, plus free bread and porter. Thomas Salmon's local history of 1913 gently noted: 'It was no unusual thing therefore for miners on their way to work in the early morning to find certain of these watchers hanging over the churchyard wall suffering from a more potent influence than the want of sleep.'

CAMELON

Anecdote only.
According to the memoirs of the Burgh Surveyor David Ronald, a man who died of a mysterious disease was lifted by James Young Simpson, the prominent physician later known as 'Chloroform' Simpson for his use of the anaesthetic. His local accomplice was a Mr Russell, who drove the carriage back to Edinburgh while Simpson steadied the body in its coat and hat.

DENNY

An excellent watchtower.
Address: Old Parish Church, Broad Street, Denny, FK6 6DA.
NGR: NS81158 82747.
Lat, Long: 56.02283, -3.908282.
Access: Steps, but viewable from afar.

Two of the three mortsafes at Airth Old Parish Church. The hinges and suspension mechanisms are still intact. *(Geoff Bailey)*

Things to see: The six-sided battlemented watchtower has a window in each face, and stands in front of the spire.

Comments: The church at Denny Cross is the local landmark.

HILLS OF DUNIPACE

A ruined watch-house.

Address: Hills of Dunipace Cemetery, Bonnybridge, FK4 1NY (on the B905 just west of junction 1 on the M876).

NGR: NS83728 81780.

Lat, Long: 56.011940, -3.877024.

Access: Park at the modern cemetery. The old walled and tree-girt burial-ground is on the western edge. It's a rough walk alongside a field to the entrance.

Things to see: An extensively ruined watch-house sits to the right of the gate.

Comments: The church is long gone but the burial-ground has a long-in-the-tooth feel.

LARBERT

The dung-heap anecdote.

Address: Larbert Old Church, Denny Road, Larbert, FK5 3AB.

NGR: NS85528 82203.

Lat, Long: 56.019025, -3.837979.
Access: Park by the church. Gravel paths in a well-kept, slightly sloping graveyard.
Comments: The church tower is a landmark in the area. A number of good stones and striking memorials.
Stories: 'The sight of the corpses had meanwhile roused the fury of the mob to the very highest pitch. They hunted the driver of the gig out of every corner in which he attempted to take shelter … The very excess of rage on the part of the people alone saved the fellow from having his brains dashed out, for in their eagerness to strike, the one pulled back the other and hindered them getting a blow.' So the *West Lothian Courier* reported the climax of the events in March 1823.

The incident started at Gilston Farm, Polmont, where there stood a huge dung-heap, a source of considerable profit to the farmer, Alexander Scott, who was collecting horse manure from the roads and supplying farms and businesses all around with the valuable fertiliser. James Forrester, Scott's servant, spotted two men digging out some bundles from the dung-heap and placing them on a gig. The gig had been seen heading along the Edinburgh road so Scott leapt on his horse and headed the graverobbers off at Linlithgow. The farmer spoke with a particular country burr, and so as he pursued the gig over Linlithgow Bridge, no one could understand his cries of 'Corrpse in the gig, corrpse in the gig, corrpse, corrpse!' Nevertheless, the snatchers knew they had been rumbled. In Linlithgow centre one of the men jumped out of the gig and ran off. The other drove on, but was stopped by the gathering crowd. Once Scott explained, the gig was searched and three cadavers found, each doubled up and tied into a bundle by a string drawn round the neck and under the knees. By this point the driver had legged it, leading to the events described in the newspaper report. It was only the fact that Scott brought the police that saved the man's life.

The three decomposed corpses were identified as coming from Larbert. One had belonged to Janet Mair, the young crippled daughter of a collier. Another was a youth named John Brown, who had been buried six weeks previously. The third was not identified immediately. Relatives reclaimed the bodies from their temporary resting place in the Town House, and reinterred them at Larbert. Meanwhile, the crowd reduced the gig to matchwood.

In jail, the driver gave his name as Thomas Stevenson; but he was in fact the notorious bodysnatcher Thomas Hodge, free again after completing his prison sentence for the crime at Lanark (see the chapter on South Lanarkshire for details of that episode). Investigation showed that Hodge had hired the gig from an Edinburgh stable, arrived with another man at a small inn near Falkirk, and went out late, returning well after midnight (much to the landlady's annoyance). This was revealing, because in the hours they were absent the two men did not have enough time to ride from Falkirk to Larbert, lift the bodies, hide them in the dung-heap, and make it back to Falkirk. They were therefore probably just couriers, the actual graverobbing and deposition in the dung-heap having been accomplished by other members of the gang. Hodge, however, did not identify his colleagues. On 2 June 1823 at the Edinburgh High Court he was accused of 'wickedly and feloniously stealing dead bodies', to which he pled Not Guilty. It was pretty much an open-and-shut case, and in virtue of his being a repeat offender, Hodge was sentenced to seven years' transportation to Australia.

At Larbert, other graves were opened out of fear there had been other depredations, but none further had been disturbed. For some months after the excitement the Larbert watch-house was regularly manned, although attendance dropped off after a while. For his troubles, Mr Scott received a silver snuff-box valued at over £5, provided by public subscription.

SLAMANNAN

Anecdote only.

Address: Parish Church, Main Street, Slamannan, FK1 3EN.

NGR: NS85611 73402.

Lat, Long: 55.940002, -3.832902.

Access: Level access onto tarmac path.

Comments: Some fine carved stones.

Stories: The 1825 Regulations for the Watch required graves to be watched for eight weeks in summer and ten weeks in winter. Members had to pay 4d each for fuel, latecomers were fined 1s, and absentees 2s 6d. On dark nights two glass lamps on poles were placed near the graves watched. Unwarranted discharge of firearms attracted a penalty of 1s per shot – in 1819 Robert Jamieson had accidentally fired his gun and damaged one of the expensive church windows. Watchers were clearly not always true and honest, as in May 1830 the Heritors noted that 'unless depredations committed by the watchmen on the Collecting House be made good the accommodation will no longer be granted'.

STIRLING

ABERFOYLE

Two superb iron coffins.

Address: Old Parish Church, Manse Road, Kirkton, Aberfoyle, FK8 3XD.

NGR: NN51845 00506.

Lat, Long: 56.174084, -4.388008.

Access: Minimal parking in the lane. Level access into cemetery, grass around the old kirk.

Things to see: 1. The pair of large iron over-coffins are some of the best of their kind still in existence. Both are set on blocks and have two integral handles on the top. In *Northern Notes and Queries* in 1889, 'J.H.' described how they were used. Two thick planks were placed in the bottom of the grave, and four strong iron bars screwed into the planks; the bars were hinged near the upper ends. The coffin was lowered into the gave, the mortsafe put over it, and the hinged rods bent over, interlinked, and padlocked.

The pair of iron coffins at Aberfoyle. *(Geoff Holder)*

The keys were given to the nearest relation. After several weeks the rods were unlocked and unscrewed, the iron coffin lifted, and the planks left in the grave.

Comments: The roofless church is in a lovely setting, with several excellent gravestones.

CALLANDER

A probable watch-house.

Address: St Kessock's Graveyard, Main Street/Bridgend Bridge, Callander, FK17 8BL.

NGR: NN62663 07891.

Lat, Long: 56.243624, -4.217741.

Access: The site is sloping and uneven.

Things to see: The fine hexagonal watch-house built into the north wall has three of its faces overlooking the graveyard, although the windows have been blocked-up. There is no sign of a chimney. An inscription above the door reads: 'Design & Constructed by Duncn McNa Joiner & Built by J.Par F.Bu & D. McGrer Masons 1852.'

Comments: If the building does originally date only to 1852, this means it was not designed as a defence against resurrectionists.

DOUNE

Anecdote only.

Address: Old Kilmadock Burial-ground (St Aedh's Church), Buchany, Doune FK17 8LN.

NGR: NN7066 0247.

Lat, Long: 56.205653, -4.121809.

Access: Walk two miles along the north bank of the River Teith from Doune, or stroll down the lane opposite Burn of Cambus Lodge at Buchany on the A84 (no parking). The site is in a field, and livestock may be present.

Comments: A beguiling riverside ruin.

Stories: On 12 January 1823 the church officer swore under oath to the Kirk Session that he would not engage in 'the raising of dead bodies in the Churchyard of Doune, of Kilmadock, or any other Churchyard or be accessory to such nefarious practices in any shape whatever.' In 1827 a stranger called Rab Stevenson stayed in Doune, and although he had no obvious employment, he had money, and made several trips out of the village, always returning a few days or weeks later. Some time after Rab left for good a Doune lad named Peter Ferguson moved to Edinburgh, and there married a servant of one of the well-known doctors in Surgeons' Square. His wife told him that late-night visitors often called, asking for the key to the cellar. One night Peter answered the knock, to find the caller was Rab Stevenson. Clearly he had been the doctor's resurrectionist agent in the Doune area.

DUNBLANE

Anecdote only.

Address: Dunblane Cathedral, The Cross, Dunblane, FK15 0AQ.

NGR: NN78120 01383.

Lat, Long: 56.189402, -3.965494.

Access: Limited parking at The Cross. Good paths. The cathedral is open most days.

Comments: The cathedral is in the care of Historic Scotland and is a treasury of historic objects and carvings. A wonderful place to visit.

Stories: In contrast with the present day, in the early nineteenth century the cathedral was roofless. Men walked the ruined nave with lanterns and firearms. When the weather impacted on comfort, the watchers took refuge in a little room in the west gable known as Katie Oggie's Hole (the hole disappeared with the reconstruction of the cathedral). On 8 June 1828, the Kirk Session wrote to the Procurator-Fiscal demanding that steps be taken to apprehend those who had been responsible for the recent violation of a grave. The Fiscal replied that he could not act as the letter had not identified the miscreants. The Session shot back a rather bad-tempered note that 'the matter was one of public notoriety' and it was the job of the authorities to investigate. There was no response, so presumably no more was done.

KILMAHOG

A watch-house.

Address: St Chug's Church, Kilmahog, FK17 8HD (1 mile west of Callander).

NGR: NN60931 08277.

Lat, Long: 56.24658, -4.245872.

Access: Entrance via a field gate at the junction of the A821 and the A84. Walk through the field – livestock sometimes present.

Things to see: The watch-house has lost its chimneystack but still retains the fireplace and window.

Comments: A lovely country graveyard with plentiful tombstones, on the site of a medieval chapel.

LOGIE

A simple watch-house.

Address: Old Parish Church, Logie, Bridge of Allan, FK9 4NH (continue 500 yards up the Sheriffmuir road past the current church and cemetery).

NGR: NS81534 96979.

Lat, Long: 56.150723, -3.908554.

Access: Park at the modern cemetery. Three steps up at the entrance arch. A sloping and uneven grassy site.

Things to see: The plain watch-house stands next to the gates. The windows have been built up.

Comments: An enchanting ruin with a full quota of *memento mori* stones and with a terrific atmosphere.

STIRLING

Site of a notorious case.

Address: Church of the Holy Rude Burial-ground/Valley Cemetery, Mar Place, Stirling, FK8 1EG.

NGR: NS79175 93778.

Lat, Long: 56.121401, -3.945061.

Access: On-street parking nearby. Good paths, level access at start, rapidly becoming more challenging as you explore the extensive site.

Things to see: The re-used eighteenth-century gravestone of Mary Witherspoon (identifiable by the carving of the Grim Reaper, dressed in a corpse shroud and holding a sexton's spade, striking a recumbent woman with a staff).

Comments: An exceptionally interesting graveyard at the heart of one of Scotland's most historic districts.

Stories: Mary Witherspoon died a poor widow in November 1822. Her body was stolen three days after the funeral, the shroud and death-clothes left behind in the grave. James McNab, the gravedigger, Daniel Mitchell, a servant and changekeeper, and James Shiels, a street-sweeper, were accused of the crime. All made it clear that the ringleader was John Forrest, a medical student who offered four guineas for a corpse and had attempted several times to coerce McNab into obtaining one.

On 19 April 1823, the Stirling Court found that Forrest had fled to Paris. He was outlawed and the trial was temporarily abandoned until the chief suspect was apprehended. Shiels disappears from the records, but McNab and Mitchell were released, to be assaulted by a large mob wherever they went. Eventually the garrison from the castle was called out. Some of the soldiers were drunk, shots were fired, and after a running riot order was eventually restored, with several injuries but without loss of life.

Dr John Forrest received the King's Pardon on 7 July 1824. Clearly he had friends in high places. Following a distinguished career he became Inspector-General of Army Hospitals in 1858 and then Honorary Physician to the Queen.

William Drysdale's *Old Faces, Old Places, and Old Stories of Stirling* has a somewhat confused tale of a rumour that apparently swept Stirling after the Burke and Hare trial. It was apparently believed that Burke, along with his own wife and Hare's spouse, had moved to Castlehill with a view to carrying on their body-supplying business. This is, of course, nonsense, as it was Burke that was hanged and Hare was taken as far as Dumfries on his way to Ireland, but it perhaps demonstrates the way that Burke and Hare quickly became figures of fearful legend, bogeymen likely to pop out of any corner of the landscape of the imagination. The Castlehill people searched

The recycled gravestone used for Mary Witherspoon at Stirling. The theft of her body sparked a notorious case. *(Geoff Holder)*

all the lodging-houses, but only turned up a couple of poor people who, for the simple fact of being less-than-handsome and therefore suspect, were instantly turned out of their quarters. Rumours of missing children were whispered about. And a drunken tailor was the victim of a practical joke when one of his friends sprang from behind a hedge and clapped a plaster on his mouth. The tailor ran home, convinced he had narrowly escaped the burkers.

CLACKMANNANSHIRE

DOLLAR

A fine watch-house.

Address: Old Dollar Parish Church, East Burnside, Dollar, FK14 7AJ.

NGR: NS96367 98091.

Lat, Long: 56.163579, -3.668989.

Access: The grassy site is uneven.

Things to see: The watch-house has a red-tiled roof, chimney and a window looking onto the graveyard.

Comments: The ruined church is in a delightful site. There is a vivid description of a bodysnatching raid in the novel *The Umbrella-Maker's Daughter* by Janet Caird.

EAST CENTRAL SCOTLAND

Who shall conceive the horrors of my secret toil, as I dabbled among the unhallowed damps of the grave?

Mary Shelley, *Frankenstein*

FIFE

ANSTRUTHER
Anecdote only.
Address: St Nicolas' Church, High Street, Anstruther Wester, KY10 3DG.
NGR: NO56444 03532.
Lat, Long: 56.222348, -2.703987.
Access: Easy access from shoreside paths and adjacent roads. Grassy.
Comments: The church tower is closed up, while part of the building is used as a hall. The graveyard has a great setting by the harbour.
Stories: One night a fisherwife heard a strange noise. Looking out she saw a man bundle a body into a sack and place it in a small boat tied up in the Dreel Burn next to the church. His cargo secure, he rowed off (presumably across the Firth of Forth to Edinburgh). Probably as a result of incidents like this, Anstruther started investing in mortsafes – at one point the parish owned eight, all of different sizes. The largest mortsafe was 7ft long and cost £4 11s. Sadly this host of mortsafes seems to have vanished.

AUCHTERTOOL
A 'janker-stone'.
Address: Parish Church, Main Street, Auchtertool, KY2 5XQ (west of the village).
NGR: NT20772 90192.
Lat, Long: 56.097914, -3.275142.
Access: Parking at the gates. Steps up the hill to the church.
Things to see: The large 'janker' or mortstone lies against the south wall of the graveyard. Thick and cumbersome, it seems to have a chunk missing, and has a hole at one end.

Comments: A pleasantly lonely spot.
Stories: Bodysnatching raids resulted in the setting up of a watching association.

CAIRNEYHILL
A lovingly restored watch-house.
Address: Cairneyhill Church, 3 Main Street, Cairneyhill, KY12 8RG.
NGR: NT05114 86377.
Lat, Long: 56.060681, -3.525373.
Access: Level access through the gates, well-made paths. Parking in the village.
Things to see: The formerly derelict watch-house has been fully restored and limewashed by the Scottish Lime Centre and Cairneyhill Heritage Group, with three windows, a chimney and a fireplace. Interpretation panels have also been set up by this splendid project.
Comments: A rare example of reconstruction and education.

CARNOCK
A ruined watch-house.
Address: Old Parish Church, Main Street, Carnock, KY12 9JG.
NGR: NT0412 8912.
Lat, Long: 56.085237, -3.542172.
Access: Steps and a slope up to the raised mound. Park in the village.
Things to see: The watch-house is roofless and overgrown, but the window and fireplace still remain.
Comments: The roofless medieval church has a sundial and other architectural features.

The watch-house at Collessie, now restored as a Renaissance mausoleum. *(Geoff Holder)*

The massive castle-like morthouse at Crail. The inscription reads, 'ERECTED for securing the DEAD ANN: DOM: MDCCCXXVI'. *(Ségolène Dupuy)*

COLLESSIE

From tomb to watch-house and back again.

Address: Parish Church, Collessie, KY15 7RQ.

NGR: NO2862 1322.

Lat, Long: 56.306002, -3.155085.

Access: Park in the village and walk up the hill. Many steps at kirkyard gates.

Things to see: The attractive limewashed rectangular building left of the entrance arch was originally the tomb of Sir James Melville of Halhill, a courtier to Mary Queen of Scots and James VI. In 1831 the now-derelict mausoleum was converted to a watch-house; in 2004 it was restored back to its seventeenth-century form – note the long inscription and the carving facing the road.

Comments: The church sits atop a steep hill.

CRAIL

A superb 'deadhouse'.

Address: Parish Church, Marketgate, Crail, KY10 3TQ.

NGR: NO61312 07990.

Lat, Long: 56.262846, -2.626142.

Access: Car park at the gates. Level access via gravel paths.

Things to see: The castle-like 'deadhouse' or morthouse of 1826 is one of the more impressive of its type, with battlements, thick walls, ventilation slits and a stout door still secured with its original iron bars. Coffined bodies were locked inside for six weeks in summer and three months in winter.

Comments: A terrific site with memorials aplenty and a Devil's stone.

CULROSS

A simple watch-house in a spectacular site, with a tale of derring-do.

Address: Culross Abbey, Kirk Street, Culross, KY12 8JB.

NGR: NS9889 8625.

Lat, Long: 56.058531, -3.625453.

Access: The site is on a hill above the village and the roads up are too narrow for parking. If arriving by car, park in the village and walk up the hill for about 400–500 yards. Drivers with a Blue Badge may be able to park at the abbey itself. The site continues up the slope.

Things to see: The small watch-house has a lean-to pantiled roof and a single window, and nestles against the eastern wall of the graveyard.

Comments: A fascinating site. The ruined part is in the care of Historic Scotland. Interpretation board.

Stories: Edinburgh surgeon Robert Liston and his companion-in-arms Ben Crouch, the notorious London bodysnatcher, dressed as sailors and landed on the shore (the boat would have been rowed across the Forth by the athletic Liston himself). After the lifting they stopped at an inn and flirted with the barmaid. But then the girl's sailor brother arrived, heaving onto the floor the sack they had hidden nearby. When the contents were revealed, both the sailor and his sister fled in horror, allowing the duo to slip safely back to Edinburgh with their prize.

DALGETY BAY

A watch-house on a gem of a site.

Address: St Bridget's Church, off Beech Avenue, Dalgety Bay, KY11 9LH (signposted off A921).

NGR: NT16935 83784.

Lat, Long: 56.039819, -3.334561.

Access: When the cul-de-sac road reaches the shore, you're there. It's a bit of a walk to the uneven and bumpy site, which has a severe slope down to the beach. The church is also on the Fife Coastal Path.

Things to see: The small rectangular watch-house sits on the outside of the western wall, its single window pointed away from the graveyard. Inset into the door-jamb is a thirteenth-century carved stone.

Comments: The setting overlooking the Forth is reason enough to visit, although having a fascinating medieval ruin and a graveyard of interesting stones is an added attraction. The roofless church is in the care of Historic Scotland.

Stories: By all accounts the beadles at Dalgety were not averse to bribes, sending signals across the water to Edinburgh when a fresh interment had taken place.

DUNBOG

A ruined watch-house.

Address: Old Parish Church, Dunbog, KY14 6JF (south off the A913 at Glenduckie crossroads).

NGR: NO2851 1803.

Lat, Long: 56.349605, -3.158632.

Access: The site is on a narrow road to the hamlet of Dunbog, so it may be easier to park on the main road and walk down and along the grass path. It's the kind of site that needs good footwear.

Things to see: The mostly-ruinous watch-house next to the gate bears a plaque reading '1822, erected for protecting the dead'.

Comments: All that remains of the church are some low walls re-used as burial enclosures.

DUNFERMLINE

Mysterious mortsafes – sadly not visible, but what a site!

Address: Dunfermline Abbey, Maygate, Dunfermline, KY12 7NE.

NGR: NT08964 87310.

Lat, Long: 56.069923, -3.463903.

Access: Dunfermline Abbey is two buildings joined together, the first medieval and owned by Historic Scotland, the other (the Abbey Church) being a later Church of Scotland structure. The older edifice is open 9.30 a.m. to 5.30 p.m. every day from April to September, 9.30 a.m. to 4.30 p.m. in October, and, from 1 November to 31 March, 9.30 a.m. to 4.30 p.m. on Monday, Tuesday, Wednesday and Saturday, 9.30 a.m. to 12.30 p.m. on Thursday, and 2 p.m. to 4.30 p.m. on Sunday. Admission charge. Visitors with disabilities can park in the abbey grounds; however, notice should be given in advance (phone 01383 739026). All paths in the grounds are accessible, while the abbey is paved with flagstones.

Comments: A visit to the abbey, abbey church and palace can take up most of the day. It's magnificent.

Stories: In 1977 several flagstones in the abbey started to sink. Investigations uncovered a void in which three coffins had been inserted. The uppermost coffin was made of lead, and bore a brass plate with the name: 'Maria Wellwood of Garvock Died 1st August 1847 Aged 70 Years.' Below this was a second lead coffin, this one encased in an iron mortsafe, of which only part survived. The coffin had partly collapsed, revealing that it housed the body of a child. The lowermost coffin was the largest. It too was lead, and again there were fragments of a surrounding iron mortsafe.

At least two of the lead coffins had been placed in wooden leather-covered over-coffins, on which the mortsafes were secured, while the lowermost coffin may have had an additional wooden box outside the mortsafe. Only Maria Wellwood's coffin had a name or date, although they were all probably interred around about the same time, with the lower coffins possibly buried a little earlier. After the last burial the flagstones had been carefully replaced, and the trio of coffins and mortsafes faithfully supported the weight of floor and visitors for 130 years, before finally coming to light in 1977.

Quite what had been going on was a mystery. How had the coffins come to be there? The burials were unrecorded; interments were not meant to take place in the abbey nave at all; heavy flagstones had to be lifted and replaced, and a space excavated to the required depth; to have overcome these obstacles and pay for high-status fittings, the people concerned were clearly not strangers to wealth and influence. And then there's the question of the mortsafes. 1847 was fifteen years after the Anatomy Act. Had seventy-year-old Maria Wellwood been so trauma-tised by the resurrectionist depredations of her younger years that she – and her family – still insisted on employing mortsafes, several layers of coffin, and a secret burial under strong flagstones? Was there still a lingering fear of the graverobbers, even at that late date? Or was the whole package an ostentatious display of wealth-in-death?

Following the archaeological investi-gation, all three coffins, along with the fragments of the mortsafes, were reinterred and the site levelled up so that the flagstones could be replaced. And the mystery coffins and mortsafes lie there still, beneath the south aisle of the nave, in the second bay from the east.

A morthouse (foreground) and watch-house at Abdie, Grange of Lindores. *(Ségolène Dupuy)*

GRANGE OF LINDORES
Watch-house and morthouse.
Address: Abdie Old Kirk, Abdie, Grange of Lindores (off B936), KY14 6HS.
NGR: NO25951 16343.
Lat, Long: 56.333644, -3.199226.
Access: From the car park of the present church in Grange of Lindores, take the unmarked lane south for a mile. Space for one car on site. A step up a slope into the uneven grassy site.
Things to see: 1. The rectangular watch-house stands to the left of the gates. Curiously, its single window faces away from the graveyard. 2. Opposite is a substantial morthouse, with an open ground-floor vault and steps up to the door. Rather than coffins, it now houses a Pictish stone, a tomb effigy and an elaborate medieval graveslab.
Comments: The remote roofless kirk is enchanting.

KENNOWAY
A watch-house.
Address: Causeway Cemetery, The Causeway, Kennoway, KY8 5JU.
NGR: NO35023 02325.
Lat, Long: 56.209073, -3.049203.
Access: Space for one or two cars at the gates, which are locked.
Things to see: This dual-function building has a session room in one part and a watch-

The watch-house end of the dual-function building at Kennoway. *(Geoff Holder)*

house at the bow-end. It can be partially viewed through the gates.

Comments: The road behind the graveyard is called Dead Wynd.

KILRENNY
Anecdote only.

Address: Parish Church, Main Street, Kilrenny, near Anstruther Easter, KY10 3JL.

NGR: NO57526 04859.

Lat, Long: 56.232459, -2.690590.

Access: *Ad hoc* parking in the small village. The site is grassy and sloping.

Comments: The fine kirk is slightly overshadowed by the Neo-Classical extravagance of the Lumsdaine burial enclosure.

Stories: In his 1887 book *Our Old Neighbours*, George Gourlay recorded the Will of John Ramsay, a mason who died in 1826: 'I am to be buried as near as may be to my mother on the sunny side of Kilrenny Kirk, under a big stone, ten feet deep, to keep my body from the inhuman monsters — the Resurrection men.'

KINGHORN
An impressive mortstone and a ruined watch-house.

Address: Parish Church, St James Place, Kinghorn, KY3 9SX.

NGR: NT27206 86930.

Lat, Long: 56.069618, -3.170809.

Access: Parking in the town. The site is grassy and a bit uneven.

Things to see: 1. A well-formed mortstone lies on the grass. A single metal loop remains, showing how the stone was lifted with a block and tackle. 2. Sadly the watch-house is so ruined as to be almost unrecognisable.

Comments: The 'Kirk by the Sea' has a splendid location overlooking the Forth.

Stories: For Kinghorn's role in an infamous incident from 1819, see the entry under Kirkcaldy.

KINGSKETTLE
A watch-house and an intriguing relic.

Address: Kingskettle Old Churchyard, Main Street, Kingskettle, KY15 7PQ.

NGR: NO31073 08304.

Lat, Long: 56.263060, -3.115503.

Access: The graveyard is grassed and level.

Things to see: The fine watch-house has a corrugated-iron pitched roof and three blocked-up windows.

Comments: The old graveyard is close to, but not at, the current church.

Stories: An iron collar that secured the neck of the corpse to the bottom of the coffin is in the National Museum of Scotland in Edinburgh.

KIRKCALDY
A watch-house swamped by vegetation, plus a notorious incident.

Address: Abbotshall Parish Church, Abbotshall Road, Kirkcaldy, KY1 1UX.

NGR: NT27464 91371.

Lat, Long: 56.109327, -3.169104.

Access: The paved path from the gate slopes up to the church. The graveyard is grassed and uneven.

Things to see: The rectangular watch-house sits behind the boundary wall, one window peeking through to survey the graveyard. Unfortunately the structure is so overgrown it is difficult to distinguish any other features. The Abbotshall Burial Watch commenced in January 1819, following the incident described overleaf.

Comments: An extensive graveyard with unusual carved stones.

Stories: In December 1818, thirty-year-old James Wilson of Edinburgh was hired by Dr Fyfe of Surgeons' Square to steal bodies from Abbotshall. The ensuing operation shows how logistically complicated a resurrectionist expedition could be. Wilson – clearly a man who knew his way around a bit of bodysnatching – promptly hired a pair of ne'er-do-wells, the brothers McLaren, who were scraping a living as navvies in Edinburgh but, more importantly, hailed from a disreputable part of Kirkcaldy called Gallatoun. Their local connections were vital to the plan. In the early nineteenth century the Kinghorn and Leith Ferry Co. ran a twice-a-day passenger ferry across the Forth, the travel time being a respectable sixty minutes, while the cargo boat took longer. Wilson and the McLarens hopped on the ferry from Leith to Kinghorn's harbour, Pettycur, made their way to Kirkcaldy, and reconnoitred Abbotshall graveyard. Two recent graves were identified and the exits scouted out. The two brothers then found a hiding place in a copse of trees nearby while Wilson visited the home of their father, Charles. With a sovereign upfront McLaren Senior was instructed to purchase rope, canvas, a shovel and lantern, and secure them in the hiding place. He was also to engage a carter who wouldn't mind a bit of unorthodox work. Wilson and the brothers then took last ferry back to Leith.

All this cool professionalism had taken place on the day Fyfe found Wilson. The following morning Wilson hired a porter – who happened to be his father-in-law, Alexander McKenzie – to take three boxes to Leith docks and have them loaded onto the cargo ferry to Pettycur. Wilson himself and the McLarens followed on the afternoon ferry. Charles McLaren picked up the boxes at Pettycur while the trio watched from the nearby inn, but at no stage were the three men associated with the boxes – a part of the plan designed to allay suspicion. However, at this point the preparations started to unwind

slightly, for there were still several hours to go before bodysnatching hour, and so the three spent the time drinking steadily. By the time they collected the hidden tools and set to work, their judgement was impaired.

The first body taken had belonged to Elizabeth Neish, a weaver's wife buried a few days previously. The next target was sailor Richard Lockhart. But although he had been buried the same day as Mrs Neish, he had drowned in a storm eight weeks previously, and in the interim his body had been in the sea – it was in advanced putrefaction when finally recovered and buried. Their senses apparently befuddled by alcohol, the snatchers failed to notice the smell. Or perhaps they didn't care. Anyway, the obnoxious odour was to be their undoing.

Although they had three boxes with them, only two were used – perhaps they ran out of time. The cases were hidden in the copse, and around 3 a.m. Charles McLaren and carter John Cartland turned up. Cartland had been told he was transporting illegal whisky, but the awful smell made him suspicious. McLaren brusquely told him to mind his own business, and at Pettycur paid him off with a measly 2s for the night's work. Wilson and the McLaren boys travelled to the harbour separately, hired a porter to take the boxes from the drop-off point to the cargo ferry, slipped the load master sixpence to ensure the boxes were loaded properly, then blithely took the passenger ferry home.

By this point the operation had involved one principal organiser, three assistants, two porters, a carter, seven man-days, four passenger and two cargo ferries, the purchase of tools and equipment, several dozen miles travelled, and the outlay of at least £2 in expenses. This should have been time, effort and money well spent, but the crew of the ferry refused to load the reeking crates, so the load master, Chapman, had one box opened. The decomposing corpse, combined with Richard Lockhart's uniform (the snatchers had failed to strip the body), made it clear what had happened. The authorities decided to set a trap. The unlabelled boxes were shipped to Leith, and, when they were claimed, Alexander McKenzie and James Wilson were arrested (the McLaren brothers, who were also present, sloped off without being apprehended). McKenzie swore he had never seen Wilson before. When told that Wilson was in fact his own son-in-law, the older man paused for a while and then said, 'You know, now I think about it, he does look familiar.' The two prisoners were taken back to Kirkcaldy, where Charles McLaren was also arrested. He confessed and put the blame on Wilson.

There then followed what was, to use a technical term, some legal funny business. As a result, only James Wilson stood in the dock of Edinburgh High Court in January 1819, where he pled guilty and was sentenced to nine months' imprisonment. The judge said he had handed down a lenient sentence as this was clearly Wilson's first attempt at bodysnatching. As all the evidence of the highly organised affair was to the contrary – Wilson was obviously in his element when making the arrangements – either His Honour was a spectacularly inept member of the Bench, or he had been bribed.

LARGO
A fine watch-house.
Address: Largo & Newburn Parish Church, Church Place, Upper Largo, KY8 6EZ.
NGR: NO42304 03502.
Lat, Long: 56.220559, -2.93197.
Access: Follow signs for car park. Steps (and a wheelchair ramp) up to the grassy sloping site.
Things to see: The good watch-house left of the steps was also a Session House, while its partner opposite was an offertory house and is now the toilets.
Comments: Carved Pictish stone and some interesting gravestones.

LEVEN
Anecdote only.
Address: Scoonie Cemetery, Scoonie Brae, Largo Road, Leven, KY8 4SX.

NGR: NO38335 01677.
Lat, Long: 56.203570, -2.995540.
Access: Parking at the cemetery. Gravel paths.
Comments: The older part has some interesting gravestones.
Stories: Another one of Robert Liston's escapades took place here, when he and a fellow student lifted the body of an innkeeper named Henderson from the local graveyard. As they were escaping, one of them fell ill so they took refuge in a convenient hostelry – which happened to have been run by Mr Henderson. The invalid was pulling himself together with a fortifying brandy in an upper room when there came the sound of a great commotion from downstairs – the town officers were searching the pub for stolen property. Fearing discovery, the students took the body from the sack, hid it, and amscrayed out of the window. That night the widow got into bed and found her dead husband lying next to her.

ROSYTH
A morthouse and several hair-raising stories.
Address: Rosyth Old Church, Limekilns, KY11 3LG (at the end of Brucehaven Road).
NGR: NT08508 82827.
Lat, Long: 56.029675, -3.469595.
Access: Park at the end of the road then walk. The site can be a bit unkempt so good footwear is advised. If the gates are locked there is a stone stile.
Things to see: The morthouse projects out from the south graveyard wall (by the coastal path), its windows boarded up and the roof grassed over.
Comments: The ruins of a medieval church in a splendid coastal position overlooking the Forth. The Fife Coastal Path passes the site.
Stories: The dark duo of boatman-surgeon Robert Liston and London bodysnatcher Ben Crouch twice preyed on Rosyth. On one occasion their target was a drowned sailor, but when they arrived they found his distraught sweetheart weeping and strewing flowers over the grave. The party bided their time and eventually the lass left, still weeping.

In double-quick time the corpse was lifted, sacked up and placed in the boat. As they were casting off the woman returned, discovered the violated grave, and her shrieks and cries from the beach accompanied the team as they pulled hard for the opposite shore. This is one of the most heartless scenes in the ghastly history of bodysnatching; and to demonstrate further how little the men concerned cared for the feelings of others, one of the snatchers had taken a flower for his buttonhole.

On another occasion, Liston led a party to lift the body of a farmer's wife. She had been a woman of great beauty, and had died in childbirth. The cadaver was in the sack resting on the kirkyard wall when through the gloom came a lantern and a dog. In their panicked exit the corpse was partially scalped, and soon after the visitor – who was the bereaved husband, coming to visit his wife's grave – found her golden hair trapped in the stones of the dyke.

ST ANDREW'S
Anecdote only.
Address: St Andrew's Cathedral, The Pends, St Andrews, KY16 9QZ.
NGR: NO51486 16641.
Lat, Long: 56.339630, -2.786347.
Access: The ruin is in the care of Historic Scotland. Good wheelchair access. Open daily 1 April-30 September 9.30 a.m. to 5.30 p.m. (to 4.30 p.m. rest of year). Admission charge. Visitor centre.
Comments: The ruins of Scotland's most magnificent cathedral.
Stories: An iron collar was dug up in 1895. It was used to secure the neck of the corpse to the bottom of the coffin. Although on display in the cathedral museum until at least the 1930s, this unusual relic, along with the iron bars of a form of mortsafe, has subsequently disappeared.

TAYPORT
A ruined watch-house.
Address: Ferry-Port-On-Craig Church, Castle Street, Tayport, DD6 9NS.

NGR: NO4591 2871.
Lat, Long: 56.447528, -2.878938.
Access: Parking on the hilly streets nearby. The entrance path slopes up.
Things to see: An utterly ruinous watch-house is built into the entrance slope.
Comments: The church is no longer in use. A number of good carved stones.

WINDYGATES
Anecdote only.
When the coffin of John McWhannel was found empty, it was suspected that the highly respected farmer had faked his death and absconded with the money he stored for the poor people of the area. What was more likely was that his unscrupulous lawyer brother Gilbert had stolen the funds, while the old man's cadaver was at that moment being dissected on an Edinburgh slab.

🦇🦇🦇🦇🦇🦇🦇🦇🦇🦇🦇🦇🦇🦇🦇🦇

PERTH & KINROSS
CAPUTH
A watch-house being reclaimed by nature.
Address: Caputh Old Church, Manse Road, Caputh, PH1 4JH.
NGR: NO08244 40027.
Lat, Long: 56.543248, -3.493834.
Access: Park at the modern cemetery. Gravel paths.
Things to see: The watch-house is badly overgrown.
Comments: Note this is not the present church, but the graveyard to its west.

CLUNIE
A fine watch-house.
Address: Parish Church, Clunie, PH10 6RQ.
NGR: NO10954 44020.
Lat, Long: 56.579879, -3.451238.
Access: Parking at the church. The main path inclines up the hill.
Things to see: The watch-house has an unusually elaborate decorated arch over the door, which was probably transplanted from an earlier building. The single window gives

a restricted view of the churchyard. The building currently stores the boards used in shoring up newly-dug graves.

Comments: A fine site beside the lovely Loch of Clunie.

COLLACE

A morthouse.

Address: Collace Old Parish Church, Kirkton of Collace, PH2 6HU (on a minor road between Kinrossie and Collace).
NGR: NO19725 31971.
Lat, Long: 56.473578, -3.309173.
Access: Parking outside church. Steps at entrance.
Things to see: The morthouse is currently boarded up awaiting restoration.
Comments: Several good carved stones in a fine country churchyard.

COUPAR ANGUS

A good watch-house and a morthouse.

Address: Abbey Church, Queen Street, Coupar Angus, PH13 9DE.
NGR: NO22330 39807.
Lat, Long: 56.543803, -3.264753.
Access: On-road parking. Gravel paths and grass.
Things to see: 1. The diminutive red sandstone octagonal watch-house stands in the centre of the burial-ground. Several old carved gravestones are arranged around it.

Built in 1822, it is in good condition, although the windows are boarded up. No chimney-stack is visible. The fireplace (not viewable) was constructed from parts of a medieval abbot's graveslab. 2. In the south-west corner (close to the fragmentary ruins of the old abbey) is a solid pitched-roof morthouse with a stout door. Squinting through the ventilation slits you can glimpse some wall-mounted memorials and a large freestanding slab that was very likely used as a coffin shelf.
Comments: A fairly extensive site with mostly nineteenth-century stones.

DUNNING

A fine watch-house.

Address: St Serf's Church, The Square, Dunning, PH2 0RG.
NGR: NO01905 14490.
Lat, Long: 56.312629, -3.587295.
Access: Parking around The Square. Level access, good paths.
Things to see: The watch-house at the gate is now used by Historic Scotland as a seasonal office for the splendid medieval kirk of St Serf's. Note the tall chimney at one end and the ball finial at the other.
Comments: St Serf's now houses the magnificent Pictish Dupplin Cross. Well worth a visit.

The octagonal watch-house at Abbey Church, Coupar Angus. *(Geoff Holder)*

ERROL

Anecdote only.

Address: Old Parish Church, High Street, Errol, PH2 7QL.

NGR: NO2520 2280.

Lat, Long: 56.391569, -3.213131.

Access: A grassy and uneven site.

Comments: The church here is long vanished but there are still many decorated gravestones.

Stories: A somewhat intoxicated local man took a short-cut through the graveyard, where he disturbed a snatcher on a black horse. The village worthy ran two miles to a safe house before relating his story.

FORTEVIOT

A good watch-house and two mortstones.

Address: Church of St Andrew, Forteviot, PH2 9BT.

NGR: NO05146 17481.

Lat, Long: 56.34052, -3.536005.

Access: Level access onto gravel paths.

Things to see: 1. The watch-house beside the gate is in very good condition and retains its window and chimney. 2. There are two flat slab mortstones in the kirkyard, one part-buried in the grass and the other mossed over, so they are not very obvious unless you look.

Comments: A standard Georgian Scottish church in an extraordinarily English-looking village.

KINFAUNS

A watch-house.

Address: Parish Church, Church Road, Kinfauns, PH2 7LD.

NGR: NO16617 22282.

Lat, Long: 56.385433, -3.352032.

Access: Beaten earth paths in a grassy kirkyard.

Things to see: The pitched-roof watch-house next to the gate has lost its chimney but still keeps one miniscule window.

Comments: Wonderful views over the Tay.

KINNAIRD

A watch-house.

Address: Parish Church, Kinnaird, PH14 9QY.

NGR: NO24303 28648.

Lat, Long: 56.443937, -3.229427.

Access: A grassy country churchyard.

Things to see: The watch-house projects out from the wall beside the gate, its single window looking onto the kirkyard.

Comments: A plain kirk with a tremendous view across the Carse of Gowrie.

KINROSS

A good watchtower.

Address: Kinross East Cemetery, Kirkgate, Kinross, KY13 8ET.

NGR: NO12826 01799.

Lat, Long: 56.200982, -3.406433.

Access: Parking close by. Several steps at the gate into a grassy site.

Things to see: The striking two-storey battlemented watchtower has windows on all sides. The date stone says it was erected in 1852, twenty years after the Anatomy Act stopped the bodysnatching industry. Was this elaborate tower really necessary?

Comments: A good collection of gravestones in a site pointing out into Loch Leven.

Stories: See the entry on Scotlandwell below.

LOGIERAIT

Three mortsafes and two mortstones.

Address: Logierait Church, Logierait, PH9 0LH.

NGR: NN96790 52036.

Lat, Long: 56.648693, -3.684823.

Access: Paved paths and grass.

Things to see: 1. Three excellent mortsafes stand within a low-walled enclosure. Two of the wraparound frames are full-size, while the third is scaled for a child's coffin. 2. Close to the enclosure are two long mortstones embedded in the grass; one still has its pair of metal lifting rings.

Comments: Two Pictish cross-slabs.

Logierait: mortsafes for two adults and one child. *(Geoff Holder)*

LUNCARTY

A good morthouse.

Address: Luncarty Cemetery, Kirkhill, Luncarty, PH1 3ET.

NGR: NO0941 3006.

Lat, Long: 56.454007, -3.471328.

Access: Up the unmarked gravel incline (immediately south of the football pitch) and park at the modern cemetery. Slope at the entrance.

Things to see: The morthouse is in good condition and open for inspection.

Comments: The church has long vanished from this midget graveyard.

PERTH

A minor watch-house but a wealth of anecdotes.

Address: Kinnoull graveyard, off Dundee Road, Perth, PH2 7AA.

NGR: NO12308 23321.

Lat, Long: 56.39378, -3.422146.

Access: Park in the Riverside Park car park next to the Rodney Fitness Centre. Sloping paths from the gate.

Things to see: The pocket watch-house next to the gate has lost most of its features and is easily missed.

Comments: A fine site on the river opposite Perth, with the consolidated remains of the medieval kirk standing on the rise.

Stories: Atholl House, a city centre mansion on Watergate occupied by Perth's leading doctors, had a garden and lawn that sloped down to the river where Tay Street now stands. The coping and steps at the bottom led to an anchoring cable for small boats called cobles. The Kinnoull burial-ground was almost directly opposite, and corpses would be taken across the river at night and delivered to a secret staircase hidden in the thick wall, which led down into a basement dissecting room next to the river. Bodies taken from other graveyards along the mighty Tay were also transported this way. Atholl House, along with the secret passage, has long since been demolished, and replaced by the Sheriff Court and adjacent buildings.

If the later accounts can be trusted, Atholl House was the centre of a small, insular, Perth-based cottage industry in bodysnatching, independent of the medical schools in the big cities. Young students were apparently apprenticed to the doctors, and under the terms of the apprenticeship had to provide cadavers for dissection. The period is poorly documented, but this appears to have been in the eighteenth century, some time before the 'golden age' of bodysnatching started around 1800. As early as the 1730s Perth Town Council passed a bye-law against

The stout walls and barrel-vaulted roof of Luncarty morthouse, built in 1832. *(Geoff Holder)*

the 'raising and abusing' of dead bodies. In 1784 the apprentices were in the process of hauling up the body of a young man when they were disturbed by a number of angry locals. On another occasion a young bride drowned herself in the River Earn. Her body was speedily lifted after the interment, so her distraught uncle came to Perth to search for it. His plight inspired the sympathy of a group of weavers, and soon a large party was scouring the streets. The body was eventually discovered in an old malt barn. The dead woman was then ceremoniously wrapped in a plaid and laid on a horse, and several hundred people accompanied the old man and the horse to their home.

As far as can be determined, Perth-based anatomical activity ceased as the major medical schools of Edinburgh, Glasgow and Aberdeen became the only places to study medicine and obtain the proper qualifications. Later, nineteenth-century, bodysnatching raids were presumably intended to supply bodies to the big anatomy schools. In March 1829 the Perth Burying Ground Protecting Association was set up, with several hundred signatories. Members could send a family member in their place or 'one of their Shopmen, or Clerks, or Journeymen, or A Substitute belonging to the Association'.

Perth can also lay claim to the 'fake corpse that comes alive' urban legend. A couple of resurrectionists left a body in a wheelbarrow at the foot of South Street to visit a nearby drinking den. As you do, especially when you have an illegally-obtained corpse just awaiting discovery and mob justice. A group of boatmen who had just come up with the tide spotted the men and removed the corpse and one of them took its place in the barrow. When the bodysnatchers returned, now fortified with a dram or three, one asked the other if they should take South Street. The boatman promptly roared out, 'No, by God, you'd better take the Watergate!' Cue, as the legend demands, the hasty exit of two terrified graverobbers.

REDGORTON
A watch-house and a morthouse.

Address: Redgorton Former Parish Church, Redgorton, PH1 3HX (half a mile south-west of Redgorton on the Pitcairngreen road).
NGR: NO08368 28395.
Lat, Long: 56.43879, -3.487717.
Access: Several steps up from the car park but level access from the lane beside the church. Earth and gravel paths.
Things to see: 1. The watch-house is in good condition, with a barred window and a tall chimney. The sundial in one corner suggests it was originally, or primarily, a Session House. 2. The stone-built morthouse is so overgrown as to easily escape notice. Dated 1832, the barrel-vaulted ceiling and ventilation holes can be viewed. The remains of an animal pen lie within.
Comments: The church is no longer in use.

SCONE
Anecdote only.

Address: Scone Old Parish Church, Burnside, Scone, PH2 6LP.
NGR: NO1154 2658.
Lat, Long: 56.414575, -3.408307.
Access: Parking nearby. Good paths.
Comments: In 1805 the church was moved stone-by-stone from Scone Palace to its current site.
Stories: It was a Saturday night on 27 October 1820 when a chaise was hired from Scone to Kinross. On board were Dr James McGregor, a young Edinburgh surgeon; John Kerr, the professional bodysnatcher from the abortive Scotlandwell case (see opposite – he had also been involved in the Lanark incident in South Lanarkshire); and a man claiming to be Major Robertson. They had been seen off by Dr Drysdale, a prominent Perth physician. At Kinross another chaise was hired, this one to the ferry-port at Pettycur. The driver recognised Kerr and surmised that the heavy trunk contained a body. When blackmail failed to provide additional payment, he informed the authorities at Burntisland. Major Robertson blustered that the trunk

contained military uniforms. However, Pettycur was a customs port so the customs officer was empowered to open the trunk. The two gentlemen were arrested but canny John Kerr slipped away. 'Major Robertson' was unmasked as Mr Ramage, an anatomy demonstrator at the University of Edinburgh. Both denied lifting the body, Ramage saying he had simply been offered it at a low price as part of his professional responsibilities, and McGregor said he knew nothing about it.

Given the social status and connections of the men, the case, like others before it, could have been quietly dropped. However, the stolen body had belonged in life to forester James Taylor, an eighty-year-old retainer of the Earl of Mansfield. The Earl's family had valued the old man as a repository of the Mansfield estate lore over several generations, and the Earl took the theft as a personal insult. With a powerful aristocrat on the rampage, there was no chance of a behind-the-scenes deal. Dr Drysdale admitted acting as lookout during the theft, but swore he had not participated in the lifting; he was not charged, even though he must have been the gang's local contact. John Kerr was never apprehended. That left the two men caught red-handed. Ramage fled to South America, while McGregor coincidentally found an urgent call to be a ship's surgeon with the Atlantic whaling fleet, meaning he would be away for two years. Both were outlawed, but in the end no-one was prosecuted for the theft of the body of the Scone octogenarian.

SCOTLANDWELL

The story of the secret vault.

Address: Portmoak Parish Church, Scotlandwell, KY13 9WN.

NGR: NO18310 01942.

Lat, Long: 56.199533, -3.312473.

Access: Tarmac paths on a very sloping site.

Comments: Just north of the village, overlooking Loch Leven.

Stories: At the end of February 1820 Daniel Butler, a former member of Ben Crouch's London gang and now an employee of

Dr Lizars in Edinburgh, met with Kinross physician Dr Glass at the home of his brother, David Glass. With Butler was a medical student who gave his name as Mills. The good doctor gave the pair directions to Scotlandwell and instructions on which grave to open there. As the duo left they were joined by the notorious Herron brothers of Edinburgh (see Abercorn in West Lothian for more of the Herrons' exploits). The following morning the body of weaver James Fisher was missing: a search party followed the cart-tracks through the frost for two miles until they petered out on the road to Pettycur.

On 5 March Butler returned to Kinross, leaving John Kerr and John Handley at David Glass' house while he consulted with Dr Glass elsewhere in the town. The doctor was not a happy camper. For a start, the raid on Scotlandwell had taken the wrong corpse, as the target (and much fresher) body was in the adjacent grave. Even worse, the furore caused by the incident meant the police now had Butler's description. Just as Butler raced round to David Glass' house to tell his compadres that the jig was up, the door was forced by the officers of the law. Butler, Kerr and Handley were taken to the lock-up in Milnathort, along with the short-handled spade, ropes, lantern and sheets of coarse cloth found with them. Under questioning, all three took the time-honoured course, each man stating that he was innocent, but the other two were the real culprits. Eventually the truth came out, and all confessed to doing the lifting on behalf of Dr Lizars, who, they all agreed, was the real villain of the piece.

At this juncture there turned up one of those anonymous letters so beloved by bodysnatchers grassing on their rivals. Addressed to the Crown Office in Edinburgh, it revealed that Mills' name was really Milne, and that he worked as a demonstrator for Drs Allan and Lizars. Milne was arrested, and after lying and obfuscating, finally admitted to the Scotlandwell lifting. However, he pleaded mitigating circumstances, stating that the supply of cadavers had dried up in recent weeks, so much so that lectures in anatomy had had to cease for lack of subjects. He therefore acted out of a desire to help his colleagues, not for money.

Milne confessed that the body of James Fisher had been taken from Scotlandwell to Lizars' anatomy rooms on Surgeons' Square. The dead man's nephews, James (a weaver from Milnathort) and George (a tradesman in Edinburgh) were granted a warrant to search the premises. The first investigation proved fruitless, but then another anonymous note arrived, with precise directions. Accompanied by a court officer, this time the Fisher brothers looked closely at a small basement room in the rear of the premises. It contained nothing except a table and a large yet suspiciously unused fireplace. A demand was made to raise the hearth-stone. Dr Lizars protested, so the Fishers replied that they would be back with tools, and the workmen might not be delicate in their approach. Faced with a *fait accompli*, Lizars acquiesced, and, in one of the most dramatic moments in the history of bodysnatching, reached into the fireplace and pulled a secret lever.

In a scene of cinematic intensity, the heavy hearth-stone swung open, revealing a subterranean brick-lined vault. Within lay the partially-dissected corpse of James Fisher. Dr Lizars was of course shocked and horrified – 'My goodness, is that really your uncle? I had no idea – I shall get to the root of this scandal, you mark my words! Of course you must have incurred some expenses: here, take £15 for your trouble … actually, take £15 each, and please return your uncle to the sacred soil of his ancestors with my blessing …'

Lizars' sanctimonious act continued under questioning. He insisted he usually obtained his cadavers from a legitimate source in London. The recent body-famine, however, had forced him to turn to the local market. Of course he did not deal with the vendors himself: that was the job of his assistants. Clearly in this case youthful fervour had led to some regrettable indiscretions; I will have to speak sternly to those young men. There

had been no conspiracy to conceal Mr Fisher's body, certainly not: the body had merely been kept in the vault because the cool atmosphere there inhibited decay. The vault, the hidden access and the secret lever? Oh, he had not installed such nefarious structures, goodness me no: he had accidentally discovered them after he bought the property. The vault was probably a priest's hole or a safehold for valuables. My dear fellow, I am an upstanding man of quality, can you not see that the whole episode is an unfortunate misunderstanding?

John Herron, nabbed for the earlier Abercorn case, admitted a minimal involvement in the Scotlandwell incident, stating he had been pressured into taking part by his brother Andrew and Daniel Butler, and had merely held the horse while the other two and Mills went off into the gloom and returned with something wrapped in coarse cloth. He was deeply shocked to learn it was a body, because he had never been involved in such a thing before or since, cross-his-heart-and-hope-to-die.

With all the gang in custody and confessions from four of them, it should have been an open-and-shut case, but nothing was straightforward in the Edinburgh Establishment's world of politics, prestige and wealth. Any prosecution would have included Dr Lizars, the prominent head of an anatomy school that was one of the cornerstones of Edinburgh's international reputation as a centre of excellence. Kick the cornerstone away and the entire edifice may crumble, removing all that lovely money. The Lord Advocate consequently chose not to prosecute anyone, and all parties were released without charge. It would be another nine years before Burke and Hare's activities forced the powers-that-be to face up to the bodysnatching scandal within the Edinburgh medical establishment. (Butler, incidentally, was later sentenced to death for robbing the Edinburgh mail-coach, but was pardoned when the skeleton of a horse he had articulated while in prison impressed a pair of visiting Austrian aristocrats. You couldn't make this stuff up, could you?)

The case still has a key unanswered question – who wrote the anonymous letters? Clearly they had a good knowledge of Dr Lizars' team and premises, so why did they want to damage him? A rival surgeon would not have risked revealing the secrets of the bodysnatching trade for fear the investigation would spread, so I suspect it was either a resurrectionist who felt he had been cheated by Lizars, or a staff member who had been recently dismissed or badly treated.

The watchtower that once stood at the Reform Street end of The Howff. *(Perth and Kinross Libraries)*

DUNDEE

BROUGHTY FERRY
A watch-house.
Address: Old Burial-ground, Fisher Street, Broughty Ferry, DD5 1EZ.
NGR: NO45898 30746.
Lat, Long: 56.465729, -2.879644.
Access: Park on Fisher Street. Access is up a tiny lane east of the Church Street junction; however, the wooden gates are locked.
Things to see: The watch-house is in good condition (and can be viewed from outside). The chimney has been removed.
Comments: The small graveyard is invisible from without.

THE HOWFF
An extraordinary graveyard with amazing stories.
Address: The Howff Cemetery, Meadowside, Dundee, DD1 1RX.
NGR: NO40152 30356.
Lat, Long: 56.461518, -2.972797.
Access: Level access off Meadowside or through the ornate gateway on Barrack Street. Paved paths.
Things to see: The brick building with a bow window facing onto the south-east corner of the graveyard (opposite the palm trees) is sometimes claimed to be a watch-house. I have my doubts, not only because it is a very unusual style, but also because there is irrefutable record of a former watchtower on the east wall. The watching association had an incredible 3,600 volunteers on its books.

Comments: A truly stupendous graveyard in the heart of the city, replete with wonderful carved stones.
Stories: The following report of a child's funeral in Dundee was recorded in *The Diary of a Resurrectionist 1811-1812*, the actual journal of London bodysnatcher Joseph Naples, published with commentary by James Blake Bailey in 1896: 'The father, in terror of the resurrection-men, had caused a small box, inclosing some deathful apparatus, communicating by means of wires, with the four corners, to be fastened on the top of the coffin. Immediately before it was lowered into the earth, a large quantity of gunpowder was poured into the box, and the hidden machinery put into a state of readiness for execution. The common opinion was, that if any one attempted to raise the body he would be blown up. The sexton seemed to dread an immediate explosion, for he started back in alarm after throwing in the first shovelful of earth.'

There is no evidence that this landmine went off, or how long it remained in the grave, but its very existence shows that the Howff had been targeted by the snatchers. The inscription on one stone, recorded in 1843 but no longer visible, even recorded the fact:

Here lies Nothing.
The Impious Resurrectionist
At night dared to invade
This quiet spot and upon it
Successful inroads made
And when to Relatives the fact
Distinctly did appear
The stone was placed to tell the world
There's nothing resting here.

One case took place around 1827. A widower was making his usual nocturnal visit to his wife's grave when he spotted a light. His approach caused two shadowy figures to flee, abandoning a lantern, pickaxe and shovel – and a sack containing the body of a woman who had been buried a few days earlier. There was no evidence against anyone, but the crowd suspected a local doctor who had a door leading from the north wall of his garden to the graveyard; the local scuttlebutt was that the ringleader was Geordie Mill, the local gravedigger. Geordie became the subject of a satirical ballad, which, if it is accurate in its details, reveals a great deal about Dundee graverobbing:

Here goes Geordie Mill, wi' his round-mou'd spade,
He's aye wishing for mair folk dead,
For the sake o' his donnel, and his bit short-bread,
To carry the spakes in the morning.

A porter cam' to Geordie's door,
A hairy trunk on his back he bore;
And in the trunk there was a line,
And in the line was sovereigns nine,
A' for a fat and sonsie quean,
Wi' the coach on Wednesday morning.

Then east the toun Geordie goes,
To ca' on Robbie Begg and Co.;
The doctor's line to Robbie shows,
Wha wished frae them a double dose,
Wi' the coach on Wednesday morning.

Geordie's wife says, 'Sirs, tak' tent,
For a warning to me's been sent,
That tells me that you will repent
Your conduct on some morning.'

Quo' Robbie, 'Wife, now hush your fears,
We ha'e the key, deil ane can steer's,
We've been weel paid this dozen o' years,
Think o' auchteen pound in a morning.'

Then they ca'd on Tam and Jock,
The lads wha used the spade and poke,
And wi' Glenlivet their throats did soak,
To keep them richt in the morning.

The hour grew late, the tryst was lain
Amang these Resurrection men,
When each his glass did freely drain,
Sayin', 'Here's success to the morning.'

But Robbie noo does sair repent
His slightin' o' the warning sent,
For the noise o' the second coffin's rent
Caused in Dundee a Deil o' a morning.

So we have a tale of a corrupt gravedigger (Geordie Mill) being paid £9 a corpse, hiring three other men, downing a fair quantity of whisky, ignoring a vague warning of danger, then being caught (or scared off) when the noise of the second coffin alerts others. In an alternative version of the ballad, the body is not to be transported by coach but by a Leith-bound ship called the *Quentin Durward*, and the customer is named as Alexander Monro the Third, Professor of Anatomy at Edinburgh University, who came to public prominence when he dissected the just-hanged corpse of William Burke in 1829. The ballad may have been penned by Mill's neighbour William McNab, a weaver and watchman. McNab was questioned but the case was not taken any further. Geordie Mill was suspended – probably because of the publicity - but not actually prosecuted for any crime. A 'donnel', by the way, is a container of whisky, and 'a fat and sonsie quean' is a buxom woman.

LOGIE CEMETERY
Anecdote only.

Address: Logie Cemetery, Lochee Road, Dundee, DD2 2ND.

NGR: NO3858 3104.

Lat, Long: 56.467517, -2.998381.

Access: The entrance is gateless and the site a substantial grassy mound. Lochee Road is a busy highway, so park where you can.

Comments: The medieval church is long vanished.

Stories: The *Dundee Advertiser* for 13 May 1824 reported that two men employed to watch a new grave overnight were assaulted by a pair of bodysnatchers, but managed to drive their assailants off. A second attack on the grave was attempted the following night, but this too was frustrated. At the time, lonely Lochee Road had a bad reputation for robbers and ne'er-do-wells.

ANGUS

KIRRIEMUIR
Anecdote only.

Betty Abbot, a widow from a travelling family near Alyth, was walking on a lonely and muddy road near Kirriemuir one dark, wet November night, when a gig drawn by a single horse approached from behind. 'That's a dirty night,' said a voice from within. 'It is that,' she replied, in her rough, very masculine voice (Betty was a large woman with the muscles of a man). The gig drove off, only to return a while later. 'That's a dark night,' said a different voice. 'Very dark,' Betty muttered. She then heard the two men debating over whether she was a woman or a man. She realised they were burkers and knew they planned to kill her. She dropped her basket and fled into a nearby wood, where a fortuitous sprawl cast her into the undergrowth and hid her from her pursuers, who after much searching and swearing eventually gave up. She stayed in her hiding place all night and in the morning, having found her basket of eggs and butter where she had abandoned it, picked it up and went on her way.

LIFF
Dual-function hearse-house and watch-house.

Address: Parish Church, Church Road, Liff, Angus, DD2 5NN.

NGR: NO33314 32888.

Lat, Long: 56.483341, -3.084385.

Access: Parking near the church. Reasonably level access on unpaved paths. Well-kept grass.

Things to see: Large double doors open out onto the road from the hearse-house, where the funeral vehicle was kept. The other end of the solidly-constructed building is a watch-house with chimney, small door and a window onto the graveyard.

Comments: Several good stones in the graveyard.

MONIKIE
A fine morthouse.

Address: Monikie Church, Kirkton of Monikie, Angus, DD5 3QN (east of Monikie Country Park on the B961).

NGR: NO51822 38833.

Lat, Long: 56.539011, -2.785011.

Access: Parking at the site. Level access.

Things to see: The rectangular slate-roofed morthouse is in good condition, with double wooden doors and a ventilation slit. It is easily viewable outside the graveyard wall, to the right of the entrance.

Comments: The church is a typical Presbyterian church in a pleasant country setting.

THE NORTH-EAST

'If any person went home longer than usual they were sure to have been "Burked" … The hair-breadth escapes from sticking-plasters, and being pursued by doctors, that were retailed each morning were truly wonderful, and timid people were afraid to go out after dark.'

William Buchanan, *Glimpses of Olden Days in Aberdeen*, 1870.

ABERDEEN

The third and smallest of Scotland's anatomy centres, Aberdeen in the eighteenth century had the reputation of a place where medical degrees could be bought and not earned. All that changed after around 1800, and soon dozens of eager students were in need of fresh bodies to dissect. The market was too restricted to attract professional gangs, so most corpses were lifted by the students themselves, with the usual degree of collaboration and corruption by gravediggers and the anatomists' acolytes.

A small trickle of legitimate cadavers came from suicides and the occasional hanged murderer, but most professors seemed happy with the status quo and the quality of teaching was poor, especially when compared with Edinburgh. In 1789 the students formed a self-help group, the Aberdeen Medico-Chirurgical Society, but despite coaxing from their colleagues in London – awash with stolen bodies – none of the Society's members could bring themselves to violate a grave. The next generation, however, were less squeamish, and by 1805 or earlier, body-theft was on the curriculum. Of course there was a price to pay. In the early years court-imposed penalties were desultory, but after a time the judges took cases more seriously. In 1815 two medical students were imprisoned for fourteen days and fined the enormous sum of £100 each.

A broadside of February 1829 told the possibly-true tale of a group of sailors who pretended one of them had recently died and sold his 'corpse' for £3. The 'dead' man was carried into a cellar, where he cut himself out of the sack and awaited developments. The anatomist soon arrived, but quickly fled at the sight of a fierce knife-wielding sailor, and soon the jolly jack tars, including the 'corpse', were turning the doctor's largesse into alcohol and good cheer.

BIELDSIDE
Anecdote only.

In many cases bodies were hidden overnight for daytime delivery, thus avoiding attracting suspicion and detection when travelling after dark. This is probably the reason why two corpses turned up here – one in the manse outhouse and another in a bakery (the baker's son was a medical student). As the body was found in a flour sack, people decided they did not want to eat bread impregnated with essence of cadaver, and took their business elsewhere.

BRIDGE OF DEE
Anecdote only.

Address: Bridge of Dee, Aberdeen, AB10 7JP.
NGR: NJ928035.
Lat, Long: 57.122871, -2.119076.
Access: Pedestrian (and endless vehicular) access at all times.
Comments: Aberdeen's grand medieval gateway, an essential transport artery over the mighty River Dee.
Stories: The bridge was the pinchpoint for snatchers returning from anywhere south of

the Dee, for it was here they could be stopped. On at least one occasion a party of medical students, with an angry crowd in hot pursuit, tipped their body over the parapet, letting the river dispose of the evidence. For an incident where this didn't quite work, see the section on Banchory-Devenick in the Aberdeenshire chapter.

DYCE
A modest watch-house.
Address: Dyce Old Parish Church, by Kirkton, off Dyce Drive, AB21 0BG.
NGR: NJ87549 15405.
Lat, Long: 57.229193, -2.207871.
Access: Parking at the gates. Level paths and grass.
Things to see: The watch-house features two blocked windows and a chimney.
Comments: A roofless kirk with Pictish stones and a riverside location.

KINGSWELLS
Anecdote only.
For his book *The Hidden City*, Robert Smith visited Gillahill, a farm east of Kingswells. There he was told a patch of woodland marked an unofficial graveyard where the medical students buried dissection cadavers. No actual bodyparts or graves had ever been seen in the soil, and, in the absence of any other evidence, Smith concluded it was just a rumour.

MARISCHAL COLLEGE & MUSEUM
A superb mortsafe.
Address: Broad Street, Aberdeen, AB12 9SB.
NGR: NJ942064.
Lat, Long: 57.148923, -2.096881.
Access: The college is currently being converted into the head office of Aberdeen City Council. When the builders leave the museum should re-open.
Things To See: The superb mortsafe employed by the Quakers of Kinmuck (and designed by Peter Brownie, bodysnatcher-turned-bodysaver – see Newhills in Aberdeenshire). It resembles an elongated turtle-shell of iron lattice-work, and formed a complete coffin cage when bolted to a lower half (which has not survived). It comes complete with a bolt-key and a 'trick' padlock with dummy key and lock (part of the key had to be pressed against a secret spring for the padlock to open). The whole cost £10, and was so heavy it required ten men to raise or lower it.
Comments: The magnificent neo-Gothic façade was not here during the bodysnatching period; the college buildings were more modest then.
Stories: Marischal College became a feared and hated place, the malign HQ of a network of informants and vultures who toured the city and surrounding county in carriages called 'Noddies'. On one occasion an angry mob assembled when a story went around that the companion of a doctor seen driving in through the gate had not been his lady-friend, but a corpse dressed up as such. Travelling folk would not pass the college gates, lest they be caught round the neck by a crook, dragged in and murdered, fresh bodies obviously being the best.

PETERCULTER
A watch-house and mortstone.
Address: St Peter's Heritage Centre, Station Road East, Peterculter, AB14 0LJ.
NGR: NJ84168 00448.
Lat, Long: 57.094733, -2.262908.
Access: A grassy cemetery with decent parking.
Things to see: 1. The simple watch-house is locked but in good condition. 2. A large mortstone lies flat in the earth.
Comments: A lovely riverside location.
Stories: It seems that St Peter's was raided by waterborne snatchers, for fifty years after the passing of the 1832 Anatomy Act, a group of medical students wanted to mark the anniversary, and also hark back to tradition – so they rowed from Aberdeen and stole a body. Not only is this possibly the latest bodysnatching (or at least, bodysnatching-proper) event on record, it is also an example of the lack of empathy so often shown by the medical élite.

ST ANDREW STREET

Anecdote only.

Address: St Andrew Street, Aberdeen, AB25 1LR.

NGR: NJ938065.

Lat, Long: 57.150068, -2.102718.

Access: City street.

Comments: Nothing now marks the site of the 'Burking Shop'.

Stories: On 19 December 1831, a mob that may have been 10,000 strong attacked the Anatomical Theatre of Dr Andrew Moir, demolishing the substantial building to the last stone. Moir had spent his student days eking out his meagre income by selling cadavers to his colleagues. In adulthood he proved to be a brilliant and inspiring teacher of anatomy. Despised by the university grandees, he set up a private anatomy class in direct opposition to the moribund official tuition on the subject, and soon attracted a loyal student following. His first school in Guestrow was attacked by a mob in 1829, but he bounced back with a bigger and better facility on Hospital Row, a now-vanished area near the west end of St Andrew Street.

But a city-centre location, unprotected by university walls, was a vulnerable site. Neighbours complained about the smell. Two boys claimed to have avoided being burked on John Street, at the back of the theatre. Burke and Hare were still on everyone's minds, and there were fresh revelations in the newspapers about London bodysnatchers. And so when a dog dug up some body parts outside the building, the slow-burning fuse was lit. The place was invaded, Moir and his students were assaulted, three corpses were paraded through the streets, fire and battering-rams came into play, and soon the scene was an inferno. Official sanctions were ineffectual, and further attacks took place on medical students and Moir's home at 63 Guestrow. A mere three men were arrested (they got twelve months' imprisonment for riot and disorder) while Moir successfully sued the council for £235 damages.

After the passions of the bodysnatching era cooled, Moir's brilliance became recognised by the medical establishment, and he ended his short life as a lecturer in anatomy at King's College.

ST MACHARS CATHEDRAL

A watch-house.

Address: The Chanonry, Old Aberdeen, AB24 1RN.

NGR: NJ938087.

Lat, Long: 57.169669, -2.102641.

Access: Some parking nearby. Flat access, some cobbled paths.

Things to see: The small but pleasing rectangular watch-house stands at the western entrance of the graveyard.

Comments: The cathedral and graveyard are wonderful, both deserving a full tour.

Stories: In November 1809 complaints were lodged about watchmen firing guns without reason.

ST PETER'S / SPITAL CEMETERY

Anecdote only.

Address: King Street, Aberdeen, AB24 3HZ.

NGR: NJ942076.

Lat, Long: 57.159675, -2.097405.

Access: Good level paths from the main entrances on King Street. Becomes far less wheelchair-friendly as you move west towards the oldest section.

Comments: A massive site full of interest.

Stories: This was one of the nearest graveyards to Marischal College, so was often hit. In October 1801 Charles Jameson, the student secretary of the Aberdeen Medical Society, was convicted of stealing the body of miller James Marr, and bound over to keep the peace, on payment of a surety of £50 provided by his father. In 1805 two bodies were taken a fortnight apart, each by a different group of four students acting on behalf of their anatomy instructor Dr Skene.

On 23 February 1806 a body was discovered in the Aberdeen Medical Society's premises, leading to a hasty after-dark reburial at Spital. The Society was fined the token penalty of one guinea, which was passed to the widow of the disinterred man. James Sangster, a night watchman in Gallowgate, sold his own wife's corpse to the anatomists and then saved face by claiming she had been stolen from Spital.

TORRY
A ruined watch-house.
Address: St Fittick's Churchyard, St Fittick's Road, Torry, AB11 8TP.
NGR: NJ96270 04958.
Lat, Long: 57.135515, -2.063259.
Access: Off-road parking. A short walk across lumpy grass. Theoretically you need a key (available from the starting hut on Balnagask Golf Course half a mile away) but the actual lock may be smashed off.
Things to see: The watch-house in the north-east corner is roofless and fairly charmless.
Comments: A roofless kirk, subject to vandalism.
Stories: The major problem for resurrectionists was that any corpse stolen from here had to be transported to Aberdeen via the ferry across the harbour mouth. On 22 December 1808 two students lifted the body of ninety-year-old Janet Spark, buried that day, but were disturbed by the minister's dog. Fearing pursuit and discovery on the ferry, they buried the corpse in the sands on the north side of Nigg Bay, from where a storm flung it onto the shore for discovery by the relatives. (Two skeletons buried at the ferry port were uncovered by building works in 1874; presumably they too were stolen corpses, from another raid.) As well as leaving the grave and coffin nakedly open, one of the less-than-professional snatchers also left behind a spade with the name Rae carved on the handle. Mr Rae Senior, no doubt fuming that his spade had been used in such a manner, had to pay compensation money to the family, while Mr Rae Junior prudently went abroad for a few months. (I wonder if this was the same Rae who later became the chief of corpse-supply from Dublin?) More depredations led to Superintendent Gibb of Aberdeen Harbour Works donating a massive granite mortstone to place over new graves.

TRINITY CEMETERY
An extraordinary modern memorial.
Address: Park Road, Pittodrie, Aberdeen, AB24 5PA.
NGR: NJ948073.
Lat, Long: 57.157024, -2.086752.
Access: Parking at the cemetery. A sloping site, with good paths.
Things to see: Dominating the extension to the east of the road is the Modernist memorial inscribed 'In Memory of Those Who Gave Their Bodies for the Advancement of Science and Medical Knowledge.' I suspect this 1960s monument was in some way an atonement for the crimes of the bodysnatching era.
Comments: An extensive graveyard split by the road.

🏴 🏴 🏴 🏴 🏴 🏴 🏴 🏴 🏴 🏴 🏴 🏴 🏴 🏴 🏴 🏴

ABERDEENSHIRE
The Aberdeenshire response to the bodysnatchers was typically robust, with a plethora of morthouse strongholds and massive granite-topped iron mortsafes springing up across the county. A local specialty was a watch-house built above a basement morthouse, although in one case the crowd of drinkers and gamblers that assembled overloaded the structure and all concerned plunged through the floor and ended up among the coffins. Many watchers were armed, but targets were not always well chosen, and victims including a wandering pig and the minister's white pony. On one occasion a poacher challenged a party of snatchers in a Donside graveyard. Seeing a white figure, he assumed it was one of the resurrectionists dressing up as a ghost to frighten him, so he advanced and seized it by the throat – only to find the white cloth was the death-shroud, and his hands were around the corpse.

BANCHORY

A splendid watchtower.

Address: Banchory-Ternan Churchyard, Station Road, Banchory, AB31 5YJ.

NGR: NO70690 95742.

Lat, Long: 57.051804, -2.484776.

Access: Parking on-site. Good paths, some slopes.

Things to see: The refurbished circular two-storey tower of 1829 has multiple windows, the round gun loop that doubled as the hole for the bellrope, and a chimneystack balanced by the bellcote. The bell, which was used to attract attention during a raid, is dated 1664 and came from an earlier church.

Comments: A good, extensive graveyard.

BANCHORY-DEVENICK

An iron coffin and a watch-house.

Address: St Devenick's Church, B9077, Banchory-Devenick. AB12 5XS.

NGR: NJ90676 02444.

Lat, Long: 57.112851, -2.155582.

Access: Restricted parking. Busy, narrow road. Steps, slopes and uneven grass.

Things to see: 1. An iron coffin lies against the far wall. This was one of two gifted by George Barclay, a builder from Cults. It weighs 19cwt (2,128lbs or 110kg), so a block-and-tackle was required to lower it into the grave and remove it six weeks later. 2. The watch-house nearby is in good condition and the interior can be inspected. In 1911 a mortstone made of two large slabs was dug up. A father had placed it over his son's coffin in 1854 – in his youth the man had been a watchman, and such was his residual horror of the resurrectionists that he felt compelled to protect the grave even at this late date.

Comments: Note this is a completely different site from Banchory.

Stories: Being a hop, skip and a jump from Aberdeen, Banchory-Devenick was often raided. In 1813 three students were caught after a tussle and imprisoned in Stonehaven, charged with attempting to violate a sepulchre, and also assaulting the watchers. Fines of £20 each were handed down, with most of the money

The Banchory watchtower. Note the multiple windows, round gun-loop that doubled as the hole for the bellrope, and the chimneystack balanced by the bellcote. *(Geoff Holder)*

used for the benefit of the poor of Banchory-Devenick parish. On another occasion a party of students led by 'Long Ned' lifted the body of a young boy, but the frozen soil shattered their spades. Pursued towards Aberdeen, they were blocked at the bottleneck of the Bridge of Dee. Long Ned tried to drop the sack into an ice hole in the river but failed and the body was recovered. And in the 1820s schoolteacher 'Wiggie' Paterson was dug up so that his knock-knees could be inspected, his skeleton ending up in the Anatomical Museum of Marischal College.

BELHELVIE/BALMEDIE

Two morthouses.

Address: Belhelvie Old Parish Church, Pettens, Balmedie, AB23 8YR (north of Balmedie).

NGR: NJ96922 19613.
Lat, Long: 57.258310, -2.066586.
Access: Limited parking. Level access, grass.
Things to see: The older of the two mortsafes is the grassed-over mound in the centre of the kirkyard. Descend five steep steps to view the semi-subterranean vaulted interior. Access with a coffin must have been awkward, which is presumably why the second, more conventional morthouse was built in the south-west corner facing the road. Erected at the intriguingly late date of 1835, it has a pitched roof, solid granite walls, and a studded wooden door secured with iron bars. Within, there was – and may be still – a second iron door, and four shelves fitted with rollers for sliding coffins in and out easily. In later years it was the temporary morgue for the bodies of drowned seamen.
Comments: An attractive ruined church.

CHAPEL OF GARIOCH
A good morthouse.
Address: Parish Church, Chapel of Garioch, AB51 5HE (north-west of Inverurie).
NGR: NJ71624 24168.
Lat, Long: 57.307204, -2.472631.
Access: Limited parking on-site. Level site with gravel paths.
Things to see: The substantial pitched-roof 'dead-house' stands outside the gates, with windows, two doors and ball finials on the gables.
Comments: A fine country church.

CLATT
A subterranean morthouse.
Address: Former Parish Church, Clatt, AB54 4NY.
NGR: NJ53873 25593.
Lat, Long: 57.322142, -2.767747.
Access: *Ad hoc* parking outside. Three steps at the inner gate. Gravel paths.
Things to see: A flight of steps outside the kirkyard lead down to the closed-up door of a subterranean burial-vault; through the barred window can be seen shelves and what appear to be lead-covered coffins.

Comments: An attractive white-harled kirk, now a community facility. Pictish stone in churchyard wall.

CLUNY
A quartet of mortsafes.
Address: Cluny kirkyard, Cluny, AB51 7RS (opposite the parish church, at the end of the minor road to Kirklands of Cluny).
NGR: NJ68462 12569.
Lat, Long: 57.201112, -2.523292.
Access: Many steps up at the gates.
Things to see: The extraordinary collection of four mortsafes is quite a sight. Each is a large granite block on top of an iron framework.
Comments: The churchyard is dominated by the charming pepper-pot Fraser Mausoleum.

COLLIESTON
A tiny watch-house.
Address: Slains Parish Church, Kirktown of Slains, Collieston, AB41 8RT.
NGR: NK04114 28962.
Lat, Long: 57.351138, -1.933280.
Access: Parking at church. The site is grassy and sloping.
Things to see: The miniscule watch-house sits in the corner of the churchyard, with a single window and a sloping roof.
Comments: St Ternan's holy well is still flowing.

COULL
A good morthouse.
Address: Parish Church, Coull, AB34 4TS (north of Aboyne).
NGR: NJ51191 02482.
Lat, Long: 57.110801, -2.806693.
Access: Parking on the lane to the church. A grassy country kirkyard.
Things to see: The muscular barrel-vaulted morthouse is built into the slope and has a roof banked with turf.
Comments: A charming rural church.
Stories: The isolated churchyard had been raided on several occasions, so at the next funeral a group of local men hid in the churchyard overnight. Sure enough, a party of

resurrectionists arrived and started to dig into the new grave. In the following tumult one of the medical students was badly injured, and in the wholesale retreat the band left behind a pickaxe, spade, screwdriver and what was probably a bespoke tool, a hook at the end of a telescopic handle, probably intended to haul the body out of the coffin. By complete coincidence, the gravedigger vanished from the district the next day.

COWIE

An underground morthouse.

Address: St Mary's Church, Cowie, Stonehaven, AB39 3RE (north-east of Cowie/Stonehaven, by the Stonehaven Golf Club).

NGR: NO88414 87314.

Lat, Long: 56.973466, -2.195745.

Access: A two-mile clifftop walk from Stonehaven or along the track from the golf clubhouse. No disabled access.

Things to see: The arch of the subterranean morthouse can be seen beneath one of the ruined church walls. The door has completely vanished underground.

Comments: A terrific clifftop ruin.

Stories: One night the watchmen saw 'something black' which appeared to move then stand still. They fired and it fell with a thud. A hit, a palpable hit! Unfortunately, investigation proved the 'snatcher' was a tombstone which had toppled in the dark. To compound the embarrassment, on their way back to Cowie the watchers met the coastguards, who had seen the flash of gunfire and had mistaken it for the distress signal from a shipwreck. On another occasion, a medical student casing the graveyard fled after hearing spectral groans – which emanated from a tinker sleeping under a tablestone.

DRUMOAK

Anecdote only.

Address: Old Drumoak Parish Church, Dalmaik AB31 5AS (east of Drumoak, off the minor road to Coalford).

NGR: NO81425 98529.

Lat, Long: 57.077400, -2.308032.

Access: Walk 500yds south along the private road from the right-angle bend, then ask permission at the Old Manse. No disabled access.

Comments: A small ruined church beside the Dee.

Stories: The resurrectionists who lifted a dwarf named Alexander 'Shotty' Ross were spotted by a local farmer named Collie. Too old to pursue them himself, Collie offered his swiftest horse to Peterculter blacksmith Charles Edward. The man-mountain promptly galloped saddleless towards Stonegavel, where he found a carriage being driven by two men, with four others walking behind. His fearsome appearance and demeanour prompted all six to decant into the woods. Shotty's body was found in a sack and reburied, while a tradesman in Aberdeen, an innocent party, later reclaimed the hired horse and gig.

FOVERAN

A ruined watch-house.

Address: Parish Church, Foveran, AB41 6AP (south-east of Newburgh).

NGR: NJ98494 24141.

Lat, Long: 57.307695, -2.026939.

Access: Parking on-site. A grassy, slightly sloping kirkyard.

Things to see: The watch-house is roofless and overgrown. One part is built into a bank, with a window overlooking that part of the graveyard.

Comments: A plain church in a quiet site.

GLENBERVIE

Anecdote only.

Address: Old Parish Kirk, Glenbervie, AB39 3YG (along the lane south from the village main street).

NGR: NO76701 80434.

Lat, Long: 56.914636, -2.384274.

Access: Good access.

Comments: The ruin of the church is at the modern cemetery.

Stories: John Clark, the beadle, kirk officer and gravedigger, was suspected by one and all of being responsible for a recent body-theft.

He would have been dismissed had not the parish minister, the Revd Drummond, discerned that the soil from the violated grave had been deposited in a completely different manner to that invariably employed by John when digging graves. CSI Glenbervie, no less.

HATTON OF FINTRAY

A good morthouse.

Address: Old Parish Church, Manse Lane, Hatton of Fintray, AB21 0JB.

NGR: NJ84071 16531.

Lat, Long: 57.239210, -2.265543.

Access: Parking at the graveyard. Grassy, slightly elevated site.

Things to see: A hulking great semi-underground mound covers a massive vault with steps descending to an iron door and a robust granite gable dated 1830. The interior was lined with sheet metal to protect against moisture percolating through from the turfed roof. Coffins lay on iron shelves.

Comments: Only one gable of the church remains.

Stories: Despite the obvious strength of the morthouse, somehow it was broken into shortly after it opened, and the body of a farmer stolen. The headless corpse was later found abandoned in a sack on a nearby road. What had the snatchers done with the head?

INVERURIE

Two mortstones.

Address: Inverurie Cemetery, Keithhall Road, Inverurie, AB51 0LR.

NGR: NJ77982 20644.

Lat, Long: 57.275492, -2.365590.

Access: Parking at entrance. Good level paths, grassy.

Things to see: Two granite mortstones, one adult-sized, the other designed for a child's coffin.

Comments: The graveyard is dominated by The Bass and Little Bass, natural glacial mounds that were re-shaped into a medieval motte-and-bailey castle.

Stories: A local person died of a mysterious disease, a circumstance likely to attract the medical fraternity. Accordingly, the farmer and a group of servants and neighbours hid on the summit of The Bass, which gave them a view of the entire graveyard. Shortly after midnight three men arrived in a trap, but spotted the watchers and attempted to flee. Two were apprehended, although the driver and vehicle escaped. Unfortunately for the authorities, the arrest was premature, as no crime had been committed. The pair were released without charge when they gave up the name of their local contact (and this only when a threatening crowd started to gather). The local lad was a fellow medical student, who was forced out of the district by the weight of opprobrium.

In 1826, Alexander Matthew was fined £20 and incarcerated for one month for taking a body. On another occasion a snatcher was caught red-handed and sequestered under guard in a small house. While one accomplice distracted the guard with food and drink, another cut his way through the thatched roof and released the prisoner. The watcher remained unaware of the escape until the police arrived to take the man to court, and found merely an empty room.

The mortstones visible today were replaced by granite-and-iron coffin-cages, but these have vanished. The mort-tackle, the tripod for the block-and-tackle required to lift the immensely heavy mortsafes, used to be stored in the Inverurie baker's shop, where overnight workers and daytime shopkeepers would look after it round the clock. This unique relic can now be viewed at the Aberdeenshire Museums Service depot in Mintlaw (call 01771 662807 in advance to arrange a visit, open Saturday afternoons only).

KEMNAY

A mortstone and an impressive morthouse.

Address: Parish Church, Kendal Road, Kemnay, AB51 5RN.

NGR: NJ73392 16140.

Lat, Long: 57.235199, -2.442420.

Access: Street parking. Level gravel paths.

Things to see: 1. As with so many other

Aberdeenshire morthouses, this bunker-like structure has a covering of turf over the vault, and a façade of solid granite blocks. The metal door is intact, and still has the great iron securing bar concealing the keyhole. Erected in 1831, it used to be lined with lead to prevent mould, and had two shelves with coffin rollers. 2. A large flat mortstone lies in the graveyard.

Comments: A fine kirkyard.

Stories: On one occasion the mortstone was placed over the coffin and the grave-earth filled in. When the coffin was dug up several weeks later, an anomalous layer of leaves was found between the stone and the earth. It was remembered that there had been a windstorm the night after the funeral, and it was concluded that the grave had been opened, letting the leaves in, but that the snatchers had been unable to lift the stone, and so replaced the earth to efface their presence.

KINNERNIE
A fine pair of mortsafes.

Address: St Mary's Cemetery, Old Kinnernie, AB32 7EA (on the road to Lyne off the A944 west of Dunecht).

NGR: NJ72478 09594.

Lat, Long: 57.176344, -2.456834.

The turf-covered stronghold of Kemnay morthouse. *(Geoff Holder)*

Access: Temporary parking for one car. Go through the signposted gate and take the path alongside the private house.

Things to see: Two granite-and-stone mortsafes are embedded in the low foundations of the church.

Comments: A tiny, little-visited site.

KIRKTON OF CULSAMOND
A combined watch-house and morthouse.

Address: Old Parish Church, Cadgers Road, Kirkton of Culsalmond, AB52 6UL (north of the hamlet, which is north of Insch).

NGR: NJ65051 32954.

Lat, Long: 57.385682, -2.581194.

Access: Grassy and slightly sloping.

Things to see: The splendid dual-function building has a room for watchers at ground level, with a basement morthouse built into the slope and reached by steps. The outer wooden door of the latter has gone but the inner iron door remains, and the interior of the barrel-vaulted space can be explored, with its stronghold walls and fittings for the three tiers of coffin shelves. Keys were entrusted to the custody of four separate keepers. Around a dozen coffins could be stored, more than enough for the rural area, so the extra space was rented out to other parishes including Banff, Portsoy and Cullen, making for a handy source of income. Fees depended on status. Local people paid 3d to 1s, while outsiders were charged between 5s and 10s. A leaking coffin meant a call-out for the carpenter, leading to a £1 fine.

Comments: A roofless church in a fine location.

Stories: A young man, hanging about the churchyard waiting for his sweetheart, disturbed a pair of bodysnatchers, who fled, leaving behind their tools, horse and gig – an expensive loss. In the 1860s the upper floor became the Sunday school, but the children refused to attend classes because they thought the place was haunted. The watch-room was subsequently used for choir practice, Bible class and parish meetings.

KIRKTON OF DURRIS

An iron coffin.

Address: Kirkton of Durris Church, AB31 6BQ (at the end of the minor road north from Kirkton of Durris).

NGR: NO77226 96518.

Lat, Long: 57.057616, -2.377821.

Access: Parking by the gates. A grassy and mostly flat site.

Things to see: Within the roofless mausoleum beside the kirk is an upside-down iron coffin. Before being brought here it saw service as a water-trough at Upper Mills, Crathes; the farmer had inserted it through a wall so cattle from two fields could drink from it.

Comments: A peaceful location.

KIRKTON OF SKENE

A good mortsafe.

Address: Skene Parish Church, Kirkton of Skene, AB32 6XE.

NGR: NJ80291 07653.

Lat, Long: 57.159308, -2.327464.

Access: Parking close by. Good, level paths.

Things to see: An excellent example of an Aberdeenshire mortsafe – a granite slab attached to a frame of iron spikes – lies beside the church.

Comments: A solid country kirk.

KIRKTON OF TOUGH

A fine mortsafe.

Address: Parish Church, Kirkton of Tough, AB33 8ER (south-east of Alford).

NGR: NJ61499 12986.

Lat, Long: 57.206007, -2.638944.

Access: Parking on site. Uphill slope at entrance.

Things to see: The mortsafe is an unusual framework of iron bars anchored by a heavy stone block at each end. It was dug up around 1906, and was clearly designed as a one-use product. Indeed, it was personally commissioned by a man before his death. Both this gentleman and another similarly encased at Alford were relatives of the local doctor, who presumably had passed on some words of advice about how to avoid becoming resurrectionist plunder.

Comments: A fine site on a mound.

Left: A typical Aberdeenshire mortsafe, with a metal cage weighted by a massive granite block. Kirkton of Skene. *(Geoff Holder)*

Right: The 'mortsafe-lite' made for personal (and permanent) use, Kirkton of Tough. *(Geoff Holder)*

Stories: Traveller James Stewart related a story his granny had told him about his father and two uncles. Lost in the birch woods at Tillyfourie at night after a rabbit hunt, the boys heard a cart draw up and a man say, 'I wonder if the laird up at Tilly's farm has got any fresh bodies for us tonight as we are running low.' The boys realised they were burkers and barricaded themselves in a fisherman's hut. The men attacked the hut with sticks and tried to break in through the roof, but finally gave up as dawn broke. Jack's sister Eliza told him another story about his granny, Kate. She was fourteen years old and camping in an old quarry with her father and mother. On an errand with a friend, they were stopped by two men in a coach who grabbed Kate's companion and smashed her head in, putting the body in the boot of the vehicle then driving off. James Stewart was born in 1954 so his granny would have been fourteen probably sometime before the First World War, almost a century after the last of the bodysnatchers. The stories are all spurious, therefore, but their persistence shows the power the terrifying burkers had over the travellers' imaginations.

LEOCHEL

A combined morthouse and watch-house.

Address: St Marnoch's Church, Upper Leochel/Kirkton, AB33 8JR (on a minor road south from the Leochel-Cushnie to Muir of Fowlis road).

NGR: NJ55152 09805.

Lat, Long: 57.176869, -2.743411.

Access: Take the private road and ask permission at the farm.

Things to see: The square watch-house retains its window but has lost its roof. A descent of seven steps leads to the stoutly-studded wooden door of the subterranean morthouse, now locked. There were (and maybe still are) three stone coffin platforms within.

Comments: This is the church at the end of the world. Utterly ruinous, and rather charming.

LUMPHANAN

A converted watchtower.

Address: Lumphanan former church, St Finan's Barn, Lumphanan, AB31 4QE (off the road to Peel of Lumphanan historic monument).

NGR: NJ57986 03855.

Lat, Long: 57.123070, -2.696054.

Access: The site is private. It can be viewed at a distance from the road.

Things to see: The former freestanding watchtower is now difficult to distinguish, as it has been incorporated into a range of outbuildings. It is the two-storey structure at the southern end of the range, identifiable by its chimney and louvred windows. The old books mention an iron coffin used as a water-trough at Auchlossan Farm nearby, but enquiries with the farmer show that this vanished some years ago.

Comments: The church is long out of use.

MARNOCH

A watch-house above a morthouse.

Address: Marnoch Cemetery, B9117, Marnoch, AB54 7RP (south-west of Aberchirder).

NGR: NJ59528 49934.

Lat, Long: 57.537719, -2.677651.

Access: Tarmac access road opposite the road junction. Grassy, level.

Things to see: The substantial L-plan house-like structure had a watch-house on the upper floor, while a flight of steps leads down to the underground morthouse. The inscription on the lintel reads, 'Built by Subscription in the year 1832. Addition 1877.' The vault, now used as a tool-store, has massive stone walls with the supports for the coffin shelves, although the iron door has vanished. The watch-house has been both the gravedigger's dwelling and a schoolroom. I'm sure attending classes above a room built for the defence of the dead would have been very educational.

Comments: Many wonderful monuments in the old graveyard.

Stories: The 'undead corpse' urban legend rises again here, the tale being that three men saw the bodysnatchers at work and one of them surreptitiously took the place of the cadaver, while the others hid to watch the fun. When the resurrectionists returned from the carriage with the sack and started to pick the body up, the man cried out, 'Let be, and I'll rise mysel'!' And so the snatchers fled, and so the legend continues.

MARYKIRK
An anatomised morthouse.
Address: Parish Church, main road, Marykirk, AB30 1UF.
NGR: NO68644 65590.
Lat, Long: 56.781131, -2.512045.
Access: Grassy and level.
Things to see: It is instructive to compare the Marykirk morthouse with more complete structures elsewhere. Here the covering of turf has been stripped away, revealing a rubble-and-earth core structure over the stone vault. The door is blocked and part of an eighteenth-century gravestone sits on the façade.
Comments: Little remains of the old church.

NEW DEER
The shadow of a watch-house.
Address: Parish Church, The Brae, New Deer, AB53 6WD.
NGR: NJ88615 46872.
Lat, Long: 57.512264, -2.192499.
Access: Street parking. Well-kept grass on a level site.
Things to see: Only the faintest imprint of a blocked-up window of the watch-house can be seen against the kirkyard wall.
Comments: A fine church with nineteenth-century gravestones.
Stories: On 18 January 1828 a crippled man named Maxwell Michael was interred. Four men elected to watch over the grave, two at the grave and the other two sheltering in the church from the bitter cold. Cries of 'Help, help, come quickly!' decoyed all four away while the body was stolen. Having been 'had', a pair of the angry watchers collected money for expenses from the outraged population, and headed by coach for Aberdeen. There they boldly marched into the premises of 'Dr B.' and, after a nuanced negotiation, searched the premises and found the body. The unused balance of the funds collected was used as the nucleus of a fund to build a watch-house.

NEWHILLS
A small watch-house.
Address: Old Parish Church, Newhills, AB21 9ST (on the road between Kingswells and Chapel of Stoneywood).
NGR: NJ87172 09470.
Lat, Long: 57.180144, -2.215231.
Access: Car park outside. Some steps.
Things to see: The small, complete watch-house stands by the gate.
Comments: A pleasantly ruined church with a distinctive monkey-puzzle tree! Note this is not the present parish kirk, which is further east.
Stories: For years the sexton, nicknamed 'Resurrectionist Marr', happily rifled graves in the company of farmer Peter Brownie, a notorious bodysnatcher from Fintray. When Brownie became a Quaker he repented for his evil deeds by designing a bodysnatcher-proof lattice-work mortsafe (the one in Marischal Museum, Aberdeen). Presumably Mr Marr was not pleased.

The story goes that, at a funeral wake that had already lasted two days, one of the company was dispatched to acquire more whisky, supplies of which were running dangerously low. As a prank, the coffin, containing the dead man, was propped up outside the door to spook him on his return. He duly reappeared freshly provisioned, but did not mention the coffin. When questioned, he replied, 'What coffin?' All trooped out, to find the subject of the wake had indeed been stolen, presumably by some passing resurrectionists.

PORTLETHEN
Anecdote only.
Address: Parish Church, Cookston Road, Portlethen, AB12 4QP.

NGR: NO92377 96607.
Lat, Long: 57.060234, -2.126129.
Access: Parking nearby. Gravel paths.
Comments: The church was built in 1843, replacing an earlier structure.
Stories: A common aspect of folk magic is that medicinal items should be gathered 'unspoken', that is, no one must speak to the gatherer while she or he is collecting the product (such as water from a particular stream or holy well). A 'skeelie' or wise woman prescribed a dish of nettles for a very sick patient, and three young men were charged with gathering the 'unspoken' nettles from the churchyard at midnight. As they approached, they heard whispering coming from behind the wall. Hoping that the voices belonged to the brothers of Jamie Leipar, who had been buried the previous week, one called out, 'Dinna spyke, dinna spyke. Ye're watchin' Jamie Leipar. We're nae resurrection fouk; we're fae Cairngrassie, come tae gaither unspoken nettles tae mak Geordie Tamson better. Dinna spyke then: for God's sake, dinna spyke, or ye'll spilt a'.' Instantly silence reigned, and the trio completed their task unchallenged. The unspoken nettles were cooked by the skeelie-wife and Geordie Tamson duly recovered.

ST CYRUS
A diminutive watch-house.
Address: Nether kirkyard, St Cyrus Nature Reserve, DD10 0DA (follow the signposts).
NGR: NO7450 6390.
Lat, Long: 56.766504, -2.431622.
Access: 600yds along a path from the visitors' centre and car park.
Things to see: The watch-house may be of restricted size, but the beachside location is to die for.
Comments: The collection of carved stones is of exceptional quality.

ST FERGUS
A watch-house in a coastal site.
Address: St Fergus' Church, Kirkton, AB42 3EN (south-east of St Fergus).

NGR: NK11560 50661.
Lat, Long: 57.545924, -1.808530.
Access: Take the lane past North Kirkton as far as you can go, then follow the path south through the fields.
Things to see: The small watch-house projects out from the graveyard, with a window in the wall. Steps over the dyke lead down to the closed-up door.
Comments: A very good collection of carved gravestones on a lonely coastal site.

TOWIE
Address: Parish Church, Towie, AB33 8RN (south of Glenkindie, Upper Donside).
NGR: NJ43968 12955.
Lat, Long: 57.203992, -2.929094.
Access: On-site car park. Level gravel paths.
Things to see: The mortsafe lies upside-down on its stone carapace like a stranded armoured centipede. This means the framework of iron straps and spikes can be easily inspected.
Comments: A fine white-harled kirk.

UDNY GREEN
A circular morthouse with revolving carousel – what will they think of next?
Address: Udny Parish Church, The Green, Udny Green, AB41 7RS (south-west of Pitmedden).
NGR: NJ88019 26295.
Lat, Long: 57.327039, -2.200613.
Access: Gravel paths.
Things to see: Unique in Scotland, the Udny morthouse is both a prime example of Aberdeenshire ingenuity, and the last hurrah of anti-bodysnatching technology. Within the circular granite walls is a wooden turntable, still there. Coffins were placed in at the door, and the turntable rotated. By the time the coffin was again facing the door, the contents were beyond the interest of the corpse-botherer. The studded wooden outer door is usually padlocked. Directly inside is another innovation, an iron door that did not swing open as usual but moved vertically up and down within a pit, sliding along grooves.

The upside-down mortsafe at Towie. *(Geoff Holder)*

The keys were held by four trusted individuals including the parish minister.

The structure was commissioned in 1832 to a design by John Marr of Cairnbrogie, and completed soon after the Anatomy Act made it redundant. Costing an enormous £114 17s to build, it was paid for by subscription (10s entrance fee plus 1s each time a coffin was deposited or removed), but many subscribers were tardy in the extreme, and fined extra. Non-subscribers were charged between 5s and £1, depending on status.

The Regulations for the morthouse demonstrated the same attention to detail as found in the construction. They set out in precise detail the exact specifications of coffin construction, imposing a fine of £2 on any carpenter who provided a sub-standard product. Bodies that were potential transmitters of infection had to be enclosed in lead or tin plate. Coffins could be removed at any time for burial by relatives, but no casket could remain unburied for more than three months.

By 1836 no-one could really be bothered any more, and the morthouse went out of use. In the Second World War it was used as a rifle store by the Home Guard.

Comments: The church is ordinary, the morthouse extraordinary.

MORAY

Like Highland Region, Moray is the land of plain and simple watch-houses in country churchyards. The one exception is the superb morthouse at Spynie.

ABERLOUR

Anecdote only.

Address: St Durstan's Old Parish Church, High Street, Charlestown of Aberlour, AB38 9PL.

NGR: NJ26347 42755.

Lat, Long: 57.469065, -3.228833.

Access: Parking nearby. Gravel paths, level site.

Comments: A nice kirkyard with fragments of the old church.

Stories: The watch-house, now gone, was furnished with a fireplace, an open Bible, a snuff-mull, pipes, a bottle of whisky, muskets, and two claymores dating from the time of Culloden. One night Jamie Gordon and Johnny Dustan were guarding two graves, including that of a woman who had the reputation of being a witch. As they opened the door to patrol on the moonless November night they were bowled over by a black horned beast. Convinced it was the Devil come to claim his servant, they fled. The following morning the culprit was identified – as Duncan Macpherson's ram.

The local physician, Dr Macpherson of Garbity, lived his adult life with a stiff arm, the result, it was rumoured, of an injury sustained when he was attacked by a watchman during his bodysnatching days as a medical student at Aberdeen.

In 1915 a mortsafe was unearthed, covering a complete and undamaged coffin which, curiously, was empty.

DALLAS

A lion-guarded watch-house.

Address: Dallas Parish Church, IV36 2RZ (on minor road south of Dallas, south-west of Elgin).

NGR: NJ12196 51823.

Lat, Long: 57.548303, -3.468934.

Access: Large car park opposite. Paved paths through the grass.

Things to see: The watch-house is decaying slightly but is still in good nick. Its standard design is embellished by a re-used sculpted stone lion placed atop the chimneystack.

Comments: A typical eighteenth-century Highland church on an ancient site.

DUFFUS

A watch-house in good condition.

Address: St Peter's Church (Old Parish Church), Duffus, IV30 5QD (just east of the village, off the B9012, south-east of Hopeman).

NGR: NJ17513 68651.

Lat, Long: 57.700171, -3.384865.

Access: Signposted from the B9012 in the centre of the village. Parking on site. In the care of Historic Scotland. Keys available locally. Telephone 01667 460232 for opening times. The grassy churchyard is well-kept.

Things to see: The simple watch-house is in good condition. An inscription above the door reads 'Watch House 1830'.

Comments: The roofless eighteenth-century kirk incorporates medieval elements, and there is a large market cross in the graveyard.

GLENERNIE

A six-sided watch-house.

Address: Edinkillie Parish Church, Glenernie, IV36 2QH (on the A940 half way between Forres and Grantown-on-Spey).

NGR: NJ01985 46579.

Lat, Long: 57.49863, -3.637577.

Access: Limited parking. The grass is well-tended.

Things to see: The hexagonal watch-house is incorporated into the graveyard wall and topped with a ball-finial.

Comments: A fine location at a crossing point of the River Divie.

MORTLACH

An octagonal watch-house.

Address: Mortlach Parish Church, Church Street, Kirktown of Mortlach, Dufftown, AB55 4BR.

NGR: NJ32374 39285.

Lat, Long: 57.438854, -3.128151.

Access: *Ad hoc* parking nearby. Well-made paths with some steps.

Things to see: The small octagonal watch-house is in good condition and has a strikingly tall chimneystack.

Comments: A substantial nineteenth-century church on an Early Christian site. A Pictish stone can be seen, along with several carved gravestones. Well worth a visit. Several malt whisky distilleries nearby.

RAFFORD

A rectangular watch-house.

Address: Rafford Burial-ground, IV36 2PT (on the B9010 south of Forres).

NGR: NJ05982 56170.

Lat, Long: 57.585733, -3.574162.

Access: *Ad hoc* parking on site. Grassy and a tad uneven.

Things to see: The watch-house (now the tool shed) is in good condition, with a pitched slate roof and two windows. It has no chimneystack but this must have been removed, as there is a fireplace within. Its foundations incorporate part of the former church.

Comments: The church was demolished in 1826.

SPYNIE

A superb morthouse – a must-see.

Address: Spynie Cemetery, Elgin, IV30 5QG.

NGR: NJ22845 65489.

Lat, Long: 57.672614, -3.29519.

Access: At the end of a cul-de-sac minor road just north of Elgin, or park at adjacent Spynie Palace (in the care of Historic Scotland, signposted from the A941, different access road from the cemetery) and walk south along the short lane. Well-kept lawn but the ground slopes up from the gate.

Things to see: The morthouse has lost its metal frame roof but its strong stone walls are intact, and the entrance gates and stepped rear ventilation hole are visible. Best of all, three stone shelves still line the walls, showing how coffins would have been stored. A sign attached to the exterior states, 'This is the site of the West gable of the Old Spynie Kirk'. New Spynie Kirk was erected elsewhere in 1736.

Comments: The site abounds with excellent carved tombstones. Ramsay MacDonald, the first Labour Prime Minister, is also buried here.

UPPER KNOCKANDO

A watch-house converted to a chapel.

Address: Knockando Parish Church, Upper Knockando, AB38 7RX (three miles west of Archiestown along the B9102).

NGR: NJ18601 42897.

Lat, Long: 57.468856, -3.357936.

Access: Take the turn-off to Cardhu and follow the signpost to the church at the end of the road. Well-made paths.

Things to see: The tiny watch-house has been converted into a simple stand alone chapel. The sign at the door states: 'The Watch House Chapel. Please Enter. And be still, meditate and pray.'

Comments: The church burned down in 1990 and has been replaced by a wonderful white building that in terms of ecclesiastical architecture combines the best of the old and the new. There are three weathered Pictish stones on the site. Distillery nearby.

THE NORTH AND WEST HIGHLANDS

The resurrectionists were at their foul work, and the graveyard, the place of repose,
was itself no longer a sanctuary!

George MacDonald, *Alec Forbes of Howglen*

ARGYLL & BUTE

In 1825 Joshua Brookes, the owner of the Blenheim Street medical school in London, received a letter from a friend sympathetic to the needs of the anatomists. According to his correspondent, 'There are plenty of subjects to be got here in the Highlands, for there are churchyards without churches and very distant from any house. I should suppose also that from the great bodily exertions which the Highlanders are accustomed to, in climbing their mountains, they will be capital subjects for demonstrating the muscles. Besides, the facility afforded for conveyance by steamboats is such that nothing would be more easy than to supply the whole London school from this quarter.'

There is no evidence that this suggestion was ever seriously considered, and the distances and transport difficulties of the Highlands prevented the area from becoming a happy hunting ground for the resurrectionists. With the exception of a few incidents centred on Inverness, there were relatively few examples of 'lifting'. Nevertheless, the Burke and Hare case caused something of a panic, with the *Inverness Courier* reporting that, 'In almost every town and village in the north nightly watches are appointed over the churchyards.' The result was a rash of building watch-houses, most constructed to a simple square or rectangular plan, with a slate roof, chimneystack, and two or three windows. Many of these watch-houses were erected long distances from any areas ever frequented by the snatchers.

BELLOCHANTUY

One of the more remote graveyards hit, but no physical evidence.

Address: Cladh Nam Paitean Burial-ground, PA29 6XB (on the A83 west coast road between Campbeltown and Glenbarr).
NGR: NR66370 34656.
Lat, Long: 55.549477, -5.705400.
Access: Park off the road and walk across the field. Uneven ground within the walls.
Comments: The isolated site originated as a burial place for drowned sailors.
Stories: In early December 1831, the body of Mary MacKinven was stolen a few days after the funeral. Twenty-five-year-old local man John MacLean was convicted of 'violating a sepulchre' and spent a year imprisoned in the Campbeltown tollbooth.

CAMPBELTOWN

Nice site but no anti-resurrectionist remains.

Address: Kilkerran Cemetery, Kilkerran Road, Campbeltown, PA28 6RB
NGR: NR72882 19403.
Lat, Long: 55.415758, -5.589933.
Access: Park at the cemetery. Sloping and uneven ground.
Comments: Very interesting graveyard with multiple early monuments.
Stories: A medical student from Campbeltown, about to dissect a cadaver in Glasgow, recognised it as having belonged to a farmer's wife from his home town. Transporting the body from Campbeltown

to the metropolis must have been an arduous and lengthy operation.

DALMALLY
An unusual 'double bed' mortsafe.
Address: Glenorchy Parish Church, on north side of Dalmally, PA33 1AY.
NGR: NN16764 27516.
Lat, Long: 56.404221, -4.971036.
Access: Park at the church. The graveyard is grassy and uneven.
Things to see: Right outside the striking white-harled church is an iron grille the size of a double bed, supported on a leg at each corner. Presumably the sides were once also protected. An unusual and visually arresting mortsafe.
Comments: A number of fine carved stones.

KILMUN
A bi-part mortsafe, two watch-houses and a morthouse.
Address: Kilmun Church, Midge Lane, Kilmun, PA21 2BU (west of Kilmun, north of Dunoon and Holy Loch).
NGR: NS16592 82073.
Lat, Long: 55.996421, -4.942439.
Access: Park at the church. Graveyard is uneven and grassy.
Things to see: 1. The upper and lower parts of a mortsafe with a fish-tail grid-design, hanging on the wall of the tower of the ruined medieval Collegiate Church. The two parts were secured with 6ft-long vertical iron rods, which have been lost. 2. A single-storey watch-house with two blocked-up windows and a slate roof. 3. A second watch-house, now lacking a roof. This was a two-storey affair, with one wall buttressed and a flight of steps descending to the lower storey. As this floor lacks windows it was probably used as a morthouse, with the watchers keeping guard above.
Comments: A fascinating site.

LOCH AWE
A pair of mortsafes.
Address: St Conan's Church, on the A85, south-west of Loch Awe hotel and railway station, PA33 1AH.
NGR: NN11595 26743.
Lat, Long: 56.395283, -5.054158.
Access: A popular tourist attraction, so there's a car park on site. Steps involved in getting around the site.
Things to see: Two mortsafes are on view in the cloisters. One comprises two sets of paired long vertical bars attached to horizontal straps. The other is of a similar construction but has a broader berm.
Comments: The church incorporates styles from almost every period of Scottish architecture. Wonderfully quirky.
Stories: The mortsafes came from Inchinnan in Renfrewshire when the church there was demolished.

LUSS
An unusual mortsafe.
Address: Parish Church, School Road, Luss, G83 8NN.
NGR: NS36100 92865.
Lat, Long: 56.100362, -4.636643.
Access: Parking next door. Level paving through the lovely lychgate.
Things to see: The mortsafe takes the form of a heavy tablestone with the sides completely enclosed by low iron railings.
Comments: An attractive neo-Gothic Victorian church in a lochside setting.

᠅ ᠅ ᠅ ᠅ ᠅ ᠅ ᠅ ᠅ ᠅ ᠅ ᠅ ᠅ ᠅ ᠅ ᠅ ᠅ ᠅

HIGHLAND REGION
ABRIACHAN
Anecdote only.
One evening a woman begged a lift from a cart on the road at Abriachan. There were two or three men in the seat. As the cart approached Inverness, the passenger spotted a toe protruding from the loose covering, which she could now clearly see was in the shape of a corpse. She kept silent and counted herself lucky not to have joined the body.

ADVIE
Watch-house.
Address: Advie Cemetery, Advie, PH26 3LP.

NGR: NJ141 352.

Lat, Long: 57.399804, -3.429549.

Access: Take the lane east from the centre of Advie. Packed-earth paths.

Things to see: The rectangular watch-house next to the east entrance was roofless until the recent addition of a corrugated iron roof.

Comments: The church has long vanished, replaced by the fine building in the actual village.

ARDERSIER

A watch-house in a good site.

Address: Old Parish Church, Kirkton, Ardersier, IV2 7TD (on a minor road east of Fort George).

NGR: NH78023 56688.

Lat, Long: 57.583591, -4.042464.

Access: Park carefully immediately outside. A grassy, uneven site.

Things to see: Good, solid watch-house with access to the interior.

Comments: An enjoyable graveyard with

Ardersier: a typical small Highland watch-house. *(Geoff Holder)*

many table-topped tombstones and carvings of mortality.

AULDEARN

A ruined watch-house.

Address: Parish Church, Boath Road, Auldearn, IV12 5SZ (in centre of the village, east of Nairn).

NGR: NH91936 55594.

Lat, Long: 57.577419, -3.808703

Access: Park by the church. The grassy graveyard is uneven.

Things to see: Sadly the watch-house is almost entirely ruined and overgrown.

Comments: Next to the present church is its ruined predecessor, associated with witchcraft.

BOAT OF GARTEN

A pair of mortsafes.

Address: Kincardine Parish Church, Auchgourish, PH24 3BS (on the B970 south of Boat of Garten).

NGR: NH93837 15527.

Lat, Long: 57.218128, -3.759604.

Access: Small parking space on a grassed area beside the churchyard gate and lane. Graveyard is grassy and uneven.

Things to see: One mortsafe is attached to the exterior church wall to the right of the door; it is a single long bar bolted to three shorter horizontal bars. The second, and more impressive specimen, has a similar form but still retains the deep bolts that penetrated the earth, and is set up on three concrete blocks laid on the grass.

Comments: An attractive and peaceful country churchyard.

Stories: A party of bodysnatchers were fired on by watchmen. The charge of small shot wounded one of the group, who had to be carried off by his comrades.

BOLESKINE

A watch-house overlooking Loch Ness.

Address: Boleskine Burial-ground, IV2 6XT, on the B852 north of Foyers.

NGR: NH5077 2216.

Lat, Long: 57.265677, -4.476551.

Access: Very limited parking on the narrow road. Several steps down from the road. The grassy graveyard is on a sloping site.

Things to see: The watch-house is in good condition but the door has been closed up because of persistent graffiti by followers of magician Aleister Crowley, whose former home, Boleskine House, is opposite.

Comments: A lovely lochside site.

BRORA

Nice site with a couple of items of interest.

Address: Clynekirkton off Clynelish Road (turn north at the distillery), East Clyne, Brora, Sutherland, KW9 6LS.

NGR: NC89499 06061.

Lat, Long: 58.029884, -3.872777.

Access: Park at the church. The site is grassy and uneven.

Things to see: 1. The circular seventeenth-century bell-tower on a knoll beside the church was once thought to be a watchtower, although this opinion has now been challenged. It functioned as a belfry until 1825 and is one of only three such structures remaining in Scotland. 2. An overgrown and ruinous watch-house stands at the west end of the graveyard.

Comments: The bell-tower, the roofless church and the old graveyard make for an enjoyable visit.

CROMDALE

A watch-house and a bullet-hit gravestone.

Address: Cromdale Parish Church, Kirk Road, by the River Spey on the west side of Cromdale, near Grantown-on-Spey, PH26 3LQ.

NGR: NJ06671 28979.

Lat, Long: 57.341721, -3.552254.

Access: Park at church. Wheelchair ramp. Packed-earth path through the grass.

Things to see: 1. The watch-house close to the entrance is a simple slate-roofed structure. 2. About twenty to twenty-five paces to the north is a gravestone bearing a mark supposedly made by a watchman's musket-ball.

Comments: Government forces defeated a Jacobite Army near here in 1690.

CROY

A watch-house in good nick.

Address: Parish Church, Croy, IV2 5WE. On northern edge of village.

NGR: NH79676 49874.

Lat, Long: 57.522963, -4.010745.

Access: Limited parking just outside. Slope up from gate into grassed churchyard.

Things to see: The watch-house by the gate is in good condition and has three unusual 'porthole' windows.

Comments: A fine, quiet village site.

DALAROSSIE

A simple watch-house.

Address: On minor road between Farr and Tomatin, next to River Findhorn, almost opposite Dalarossie Cottage, IV13 7YA .

NGR: NH76701 24198.

Lat, Long: 57.291671, -4.047489.

Access: Limited parking on the track from the road to the church. Grassy.

Things to see: Unusually, the watch-house is butted on to the end of the church, which may mean that this simple white-harled structure was multi-functional.

Comments: The church is plain but has a pleasant setting close to the river.

DORES

From bodysnatching to Sunday school.

Address: Parish Church, Dores, IV2 6TQ.

NGR: NH60097 35019.

Lat, Long: 57.384078, -4.328911.

Access: Parking outside. Paved and gravel path.

Things to see: 1. The simple rectangular watch-house at the gate has been converted for use as a Session House and Sunday school. 2. An oblong mortstone lies against the graveyard wall.

Comments: A fine graveyard with impressive war memorial entrance gate.

DRUMNADROCHIT

A watch-house in a fine site.

Address: Old Kilmore Graveyard, Lewiston, Drumnadrochit, IV63 6UF (just past the Benleva Hotel on Kilmore Road).

The watch-house at Dores is now a Sunday school. The window is modern. *(Geoff Holder)*

A caged roof on a lair at Glen Convinth. *(Geoff Holder)*

NGR: NH51548 29565.
Lat, Long: 57.332351, -4.467663.
Access: Park next to graveyard or at the hotel. Well-kept grass.
Things to see: The small watch-house is a standard Highland design, with a rectangular rubble construction, slate roof and chimney.
Comments: An interesting graveyard with the ivy-clad ruins of the former church.

DUNLICHITY
A good watch-house.
Address: Parish Church, Dunlichity, IV2 6AN (west of Farr).
NGR: NH65976 32969.
Lat, Long: 57.367395, -4.230015.
Access: *Ad hoc* parking on narrow roads around church. Entrance is a grassy slope, and the interior rises up to rocky outcrops.
Things to see: 1. The watch-house next to the gate is in good condition and the door from the road is sometimes open. The arrangement of the windows – two above, one below – suggests there was a temporary floor or platform at the upper level, making it almost a watchtower. 2. One of the gravestones is supposed to bear the marks of pellets from a gun fired by a watchman. The wounds may have been covered over by moss.

Comments: One of those country churches that just oozes history.

GLEN CONVINTH
An excellent caged lair.
Address: Glen Convinth Former Parish Church, Convinth, IV4 7HS (on the A833 south of Kiltarlity).
NGR: NH5120 3746.
Lat, Long: 57.403157, -4.478121.
Access: Pull off west on the track just south of White Bridge junction. Walk up track (slight slope). Site is grassy and uneven.
Things to see: A low stone lair with a pitched iron framework roof.
Comments: Little visited and lovely.
Stories: The story goes that a bodysnatcher was buried somewhere near the tree in the centre of the churchyard – and that as divine punishment for his crimes, his bones kept rising to the surface.

GLEN URQUHART
A fine mortsafe.
Address: St Ninian's Episcopal Church, Glen Urquhart, IV63 6TJ (west of Balnain on the A831).
NGR: NH43127 30427.
Lat, Long: 57.337339, -4.607875.

Access: Parking at the church. Well-kept grass on slightly sloping site.

Things to see: A metal mortsafe sits in the graveyard, its shape that of a cylinder cut in half along the long axis.

Comments: An attractive white-painted church overlooking Loch Meiklie.

INVERNESS
Portrait of an alleged resurrectionist.

Address: Inverness Town House, High Street, Inverness, IV1 1JJ.

NGR: NH666451.

Lat, Long: 57.477270, -4.224986.

Access: Highland Council offices. Open normal office hours Monday to Friday, entry free. Entrance on Castle Street. Lift for access to upper floors.

Things to see: Portrait of Dr John Inglis Nicol (1788-1849), Provost of Inverness 1840-1843. Painted by Robert Innes of Edinburgh, it hangs in the Main Hall.

Comments: An imposing late-Victorian municipal building, replete with paintings and artefacts from the city's past.

Stories: Dr Nicol was educated in Inverness, London and Germany before returning to his home city in 1812 to take up a position as a medical practitioner. Deeply interested in public health, he improved the sewage and sanitary systems, and died dealing with a cholera epidemic. A stalwart of municipal respectability, there was also a persistent rumour that he was involved in resurrectionist activities, although whether for his own anatomical practice or to supply his colleagues in Aberdeen is not clear.

The best-known story about Dr Nicol is that one of his children died and was buried in a grave next to that of another child. After the funeral the doctor was seen to place something on the second grave. The child's father was suspicious and so returned after dark, to find a luminous mark on the gravestone. He moved the mark onto the grave of the doctor's child, and later that night Nicol and an associate opened the marked grave. Back in the anatomy room, the good doctor was faced with the enormity of his deed when he came face-to-face with his own offspring. With its mysterious (and unexplained) luminous mark and the terrible retributive fate, there may be an element of exaggeration, even folklore, about the tale. In one even-more-Gothic version, Nicol's wife recognised the child's discarded clothes outside the anatomy room door, realised that her husband was about to dissect her own flesh and blood, and died of the shock. On the other hand, there could be an element of truth to the story…

INVERNESS – CHAPELYARD CEMETERY
Was this bodysnatching central in Inverness?

Address: Chapel Street, Inverness, IV1 1NA

NGR: NH664456.

Lat, Long: 57.481052, -4.229087.

Access: The cemetery is locked most of the time.

Comments: This large graveyard has many carved stones. The paths were laid over the graves of the cholera victims.

Stories: If the story of Dr Nicol lifting a child's body is true, it probably took place in this extensive city cemetery. In 1829 an old woman was buried. She was too poor to have a legacy or friends to pay for the watch, so the grave was left unguarded and her body was stolen on the night of the funeral. A short while later, another old woman with no friends was buried. This time a few local people decided to mount a watch, but they were too late in applying for permission and so could not get admission to the churchyard. Nevertheless they patrolled the streets the night she was buried, and scared away a quartet of snatchers. The following night, however, no guard was set, and consequently the beldame's corpse was stolen. If we can assume Dr Nicol was somehow involved in these cases, he obviously had accomplices. Were they visitors from Aberdeen, or local men?

The two-storey watch-house at Petty, built in 1825. Note the diminutive windows. *(Geoff Holder)*

KILMONIVAIG

Shooting at a gravestone.

Address: Parish Church, Kilmonivaig, PH34 4EN (on the A82 at the north-west edge of Spean Bridge).

NGR: NN21283 81933.

Lat, Long: 56.894203, -4.935674.

Access: Park outside, level access, grassy surface.

Comments: A lovely and peaceful country churchyard.

Stories: The sexton mistakenly thought he saw a party of resurrectionists and let off a shot: he hit a gravestone.

KIRKHILL

'Is it my imagination or is this body still warm?'

Address: Kirkhill Graveyard (former Wardlaw Parish Church), Wardlaw Road, Kirkhill, IV5 7NB.

NGR: NH54967 45705.

Lat, Long: 57.478323, -4.420454.

Access: Park nearby. One step before and two steps after the gate. Grassy with the occasional slope.

Comments: The former church is worth a visit.

Stories: The story goes that a pair of bodysnatchers paused for a wee drink at the Bogroy Inn, which still stands on the A862-B9164 junction. The local magistrate quickly changed places with the corpse left sitting on the carriage seat. On continuing their journey one of the resurrectionists said, 'Is it my imagination or is this body still warm?' The 'corpse' promptly replied, 'You would be warm too if you had to sit out in this sun with not a drop to drink.' Cue, as tradition demands, a hasty exit by two terrified graverobbers. The same story is told at Eckford at the opposite end of Scotland.

MOY

A Highland watch-house.
Address: Parish Church, Moy, B9154 (off A9), on western shore of Loch Moy, IV13 7YE.
NGR: NH77195 34213.
Lat, Long: 57.381709, -4.044289.
Access: Take driveway from road and park at church. Three steps up to graveyard gate. Uneven grass.
Things to see: The plain three-windowed watch-house stands next to the entrance.
Comments: A plain church in an attractive setting.

NAIRN

Anecdote only.
Address: Former Parish Church, Church Road (off Mill Road), Nairn, IV12 4AW.
NGR: NH88530 56283.
Lat, Long: 57.582787, -3.865941.
Access: Parking in the town. Well-kept grass.
Comments: The church is a consolidated ruin.
Stories: The relatives of a just-buried child returned to visit the grave on the evening of the funeral, only to find four men attempting to disinter the body. The group were chased off, but were still hanging around the following day, so an overnight watch was mounted. The curious thing about this episode is that it took place in June 1844, a full twelve years after bodysnatching ceased to be a necessity for anatomical subjects, all of which suggests something out of the ordinary was going on.

PETTY

A good watch-house.
Address: Old Petty Parish Church, Petty, IV2 7JH (north of Castle Stuart on the B9039 road to Ardersier).
NGR: NH73871 49886.
Lat, Long: 57.521544, -4.107563.
Access: Limited parking in the lane. Some steps, gravel paths, and sloping ground.
Things to see: The watch-house built into a slope is in good condition.
Comments: The church is closed but the graveyard is full of interesting memorials.

ROGART

A standard watch-house.
Address: St Callan's Church, Rogart, on a minor road between Pittentrail and Rhilochan, off A839, west of Golspie, IV28 3YD.
NGR: NC73874 03521.
Lat, Long: 58.002915, -4.135796.
Access: Park carefully in the lane off the road. Good tarmac path.
Things to see: A typical, simple Highland watch-house stands next to the gate. The structure is in good condition.
Comments: Expansive views.

ROBERT LOUIS STEVENSON'S 'THE BODY-SNATCHER'

> 'If the reader is inclined for further particulars on this not particularly cheerful subject, he will find them in a short story by Robert Louis Stevenson called 'The Body-Snatcher', but it may be suggested that it would be wise for an imaginative individual not to read it just before retiring.'
>
> Frederick W. Watkeys, *Old Edinburgh*, 1908

Stevenson's story was written at Kinnaird Cottage in Pitlochry, Perthshire, in June 1881. It languished for a few years, possibly because the writer thought it was too grotesque (he wrote he had 'long condemned the story as an offence against good manners'). It finally saw print in the *Pall Mall* Christmas 'Extra' for 1884 and again in the *Pall Mall Gazette* on 31 January and 1 February 1885. He was paid £30 for it (the equivalent of three decent corpses during the bodysnatching years). The advertising campaign – on sandwich-boards paraded through London – was suppressed by the police on grounds of good taste. The publication came between *Treasure Island* and *The Strange Case of Dr Jekyll and Mr Hyde*, and can be seen as a precursor of the latter immortal tale of horror.

In 1945 the story was adapted into an atmospheric black-and-white film, with Boris Karloff as murderous cabman John Gray supplying bodies to Dr Wolfe Macfarlane (played by Henry Daniell). Fans of classic horror cinema will need no further recommendation when they learn *The Body Snatcher* was produced and co-scripted by Val Newton, directed by Robert Wise, and has a cameo by Bela Lugosi. The terrific taglines for the film included: The Unholiest Partnership This Side of the Grave! Not Hollywood Bunk – But Dramatized From Unthinkable FACTS of Record! Foul Traffic in Dead Bodies! Foul Fingers Crimson with Dead Men's Blood!'

Stevenson's original discusses Mr K----, 'a certain extramural teacher of anatomy', a clear allusion to Dr Robert Knox, and likewise the film, set in 1831, makes several direct references to the Burke and Hare story. As for the location, Stevenson knew Glencorse well (see the Midlothian chapter), and even wrote to a friend that he might appear there after his death.

So sit back and enjoy this classic slice of sinister literature. But as the man said, imaginative individuals should exercise caution before bedtime…

THE BODY-SNATCHER

by Robert Louis Stevenson

Every night in the year, four of us sat in the small parlour of the George at Debenham – the undertaker, and the landlord, and Fettes, and myself. Sometimes there would be more; but blow high, blow low, come rain or snow or frost, we four would be each planted in his own particular arm-chair. Fettes was an old drunken Scotchman, a man of education obviously, and a man of some property, since he lived in idleness. He had come to Debenham years ago, while still young, and by a mere continuance of living had grown to be an adopted townsman. His blue camlet cloak was a local antiquity, like the church-spire. His place in the parlour at the George, his absence from church, his old, crapulous, disreputable vices, were all things of course in Debenham. He had some vague Radical opinions and some fleeting infidelities, which he would now and again set forth and emphasise with tottering slaps upon the table. He drank rum – five glasses regularly every evening; and for the greater portion of his nightly visit to the George sat, with his glass in his right hand, in a state of melancholy alcoholic saturation. We called him the Doctor, for he was supposed to have some special knowledge of medicine, and had been known, upon a pinch, to set a fracture or reduce a dislocation; but beyond these slight particulars, we had no knowledge of his character and antecedents.

One dark winter night – it had struck nine some time before the landlord joined us – there was a sick man in the George, a great neighbouring proprietor suddenly struck down with apoplexy on his way to Parliament; and the great man's still greater London doctor had been telegraphed to his bedside. It was the first time that such a thing had happened in Debenham, for the railway was but newly open, and we were all proportionately moved by the occurrence.

'He's come,' said the landlord, after he had filled and lighted his pipe.

'He?' said I. 'Who? – not the doctor?'

'Himself,' replied our host.

'What is his name?'

'Dr Macfarlane,' said the landlord.

Fettes was far through his third tumblers stupidly fuddled, now nodding over, now staring mazily around him; but at the last word he seemed to awaken, and repeated the name 'Macfarlane' twice, quietly enough the first time, but with sudden emotion at the second.

'Yes,' said the landlord, 'that's his name, Doctor Wolfe Macfarlane.'

Fettes became instantly sober; his eyes awoke, his voice became clear, loud, and steady, his language forcible and earnest. We were all startled by the transformation, as if a man had risen from the dead.

'I beg your pardon,' he said. 'I am afraid I have not been paying much attention to your talk. Who is this Wolfe Macfarlane?' And then, when he had heard the landlord out, 'It cannot be, it cannot be,' he added; 'and yet I would like well to see him face to face.'

'Do you know him, Doctor?' asked the undertaker, with a gasp.

'God forbid!' was the reply. 'And yet the name is a strange one; it were too much to fancy two. Tell me, landlord, is he old?'

'Well,' said the host, 'he's not a young man, to be sure, and his hair is white; but he looks younger than you.'

'He is older, though; years older. But,' with a slap upon the table, 'it's the rum you see in my face – rum and sin. This man, perhaps, may have an easy conscience and a good digestion. Conscience! Hear me speak. You would think I was some good, old, decent Christian, would you not? But no, not I; I never canted. Voltaire might have canted if he'd stood in my shoes; but the brains' – with a rattling fillip on his bald head – 'the brains were clear and active, and I saw and made no deductions.'

'If you know this doctor,' I ventured to remark, after a somewhat awful pause, 'I should gather that you do not share the landlord's good opinion.'

Fettes paid no regard to me.

'Yes,' he said, with sudden decision, 'I must see him face to face.'

There was another pause, and then a door was closed rather sharply on the first floor, and a step was heard upon the stair.

'That's the doctor,' cried the landlord. 'Look sharp, and you can catch him.'

It was but two steps from the small parlour to the door of the old George Inn; the wide oak staircase landed almost in the street; there was room for a Turkey rug and nothing more between the threshold and the last round of the descent; but this little space was every evening brilliantly lit up, not only by the light upon the stair and the great signal-lamp below the sign, but by the warm radiance of the barroom window. The George thus brightly advertised itself to passers-by in the cold street. Fettes walked steadily to the spot, and we, who were hanging behind, beheld the two men meet, as one of them had phrased it, face to face. Dr Macfarlane was alert and vigorous. His white hair set off his pale and placid, although energetic, countenance. He was richly dressed in the finest of broadcloth and the whitest of linen, with a great gold watch-chain, and studs and spectacles of the same precious material. He wore a broad-folded tie, white and speckled with lilac, and he carried on his arm a comfortable driving-coat of fur. There was no doubt but he became his years, breathing, as he did, of wealth and consideration; and it was a surprising contrast to see our parlour sot – bald, dirty, pimpled, and robed in his old camlet cloak – confront him at the bottom of the stairs.

'Macfarlane!' he said somewhat loudly, more like a herald than a friend.

The great doctor pulled up short on the fourth step, as though the familiarity of the address surprised and somewhat shocked his dignity.

'Toddy Macfarlane!' repeated Fettes.

The London man almost staggered. He stared for the swiftest of seconds at the man before him, glanced behind him with a sort of scare, and then in a startled whisper 'Fettes!' he said, 'you!'

'Ay,' said the other, 'me! Did you think I was dead too? We are not so easy shut of our acquaintance.'

'Hush, hush!' exclaimed the doctor. 'Hush, hush! this meeting is so unexpected – I can see you are unmanned. I hardly knew you, I confess, at first; but I am overjoyed – overjoyed to have this opportunity. For the present it must be how-d'ye-do and good-by in one, for my fly is waiting, and I must not fail the train; but you shall – let me see – yes – you shall give me your address, and you can count on early news of me. We must do something for you, Fettes. I fear you are out at elbows; but we must see to that for auld lang syne, as once we sang at suppers.'

'Money!' cried Fettes; 'money from you! The money that I had from you is lying where I cast it in the rain.'

Dr Macfarlane had talked himself into some measure of superiority and confidence, but the uncommon energy of this refusal cast him back into his first confusion.

A horrible, ugly look came and went across his almost venerable countenance. 'My dear fellow,' he said, 'be it as you please; my last thought is to offend you. I would intrude on none. I will leave you my address however—.'

'I do not wish it – I do not wish to know the roof that shelters you,' interrupted the other. 'I heard your name; I feared it might be you; I wished to know if, after all, there were a God; I know now that there is none. Begone!'

He still stood in the middle of the rug, between the stair and doorway; and the great London physician, in order to escape, would be forced to step to one side. It was plain that he hesitated before the thought of this humiliation. White as he was, there was a dangerous glitter in his spectacles; but while he still paused uncertain, he became aware that the driver of his fly was peering in from the street at this unusual scene, and caught a glimpse at the same time of our little body from the parlour, huddled by the corner of the bar. The presence of so many witnesses decided him at once to flee. He crouched together, brushing on the wainscot, and made a dart like a serpent, striking for the door. But his tribulation was not yet entirely at an end, for even as he was passing Fettes clutched him by the arm and these words came in a whisper, and yet painfully distinct, 'Have you seen it again?'

The great rich London doctor cried out aloud with a sharp, throttling cry; he dashed his questioner across the open space, and, with his hands over his head, fled out of the door like a detected thief. Before it had occurred to one of us to make a movement the fly was already rattling toward the station. The scene was over like a dream, but the dream had left proofs and traces of its passage. Next day the servant found the fine gold spectacles broken on the threshold, and that very night we were all standing breathless by the barroom window, and Fettes at our side, sober, pale and resolute in look.

'God protect us, Mr Fettes!' said the landlord, coming first into possession of his customary senses. 'What in the universe is all this? These are strange things you have been saying.'

Fettes turned toward us; he looked us each in succession in the face. 'See if you can hold your tongues,' said he. 'That man Macfarlane is not safe to cross; those that have done so already have repented it too late.'

And then, without so much as finishing his third glass, far less waiting for the other two, he bade us good-by and went forth, under the lamp of the hotel, into the black night.

We three turned to our places in the parlour, with the big red fire and four clear candles; and as we recapitulated what had passed the first chill of our surprise soon changed into a glow of curiosity. We sat late; it was the latest session I have known in the old George. Each man, before we parted, had his theory that he was bound to prove; and none of us had any nearer business in this world than to track out the past of our condemned companion, and surprise the secret that he shared with the great London doctor. It is no great boast, but I believe I was a better hand at worming out a story than either of my fellows at the George; and perhaps there is now no other man alive who could narrate to you the following foul and unnatural events.

In his young days Fettes studied medicine in the schools of Edinburgh. He had talent of a kind, the talent that picks up swiftly what it hears and readily retails it for its own. He worked little at home; but he was civil, attentive, and intelligent in the presence of his masters. They soon picked him out as a lad who listened closely and remembered well; nay, strange as it seemed to me when I first heard it, he was in those days well favoured, and pleased by his exterior. There was, at that period, a certain extramural teacher of anatomy, whom I shall here designate by the letter K. His name was subsequently too well known. The man who bore it skulked through the streets of Edinburgh in disguise, while the mob that applauded at the execution of Burke called loudly for the blood of his employer. But Mr K— was then at the top of his vogue; he enjoyed a popularity due partly to his own talent and address, partly to the incapacity of his rival, the university professor. The students, at least, swore by his name, and Fettes believed himself, and was believed by others, to have laid the foundations of success when he had acquired the favour of this meteorically famous man. Mr K— was a *bon vivant* as well as an accomplished teacher; he liked a sly allusion no less than a careful preparation. In both capacities Fettes enjoyed and deserved his notice, and by the second year of his attendance he held the half-regular position of second demonstrator or sub-assistant in his class.

In this capacity, the charge of the theatre and lecturerdom devolved in particular upon his shoulders. He had to answer for the cleanliness of the premises and the conduct of the other students, and it was a part of his duty to supply, receive, and divide the various subjects. It was with a view to this last – at that time very delicate – affair that he was lodged by Mr K— in the same wynd, and at last in the same building, with the dissecting-room. Here, after a night of turbulent pleasures, his hand still tottering, his sight still misty and confused, he would be called out of bed in the black hours before the winter dawn by the unclean and desperate interlopers who supplied the table. He would open the door to these men, since infamous throughout the land. He would help them with their tragic burden, pay them their sordid price, and remain alone, when they were gone, with the unfriendly relics of humanity. From such a scene he would return to snatch another hour or two of slumber, to repair the abuses of the night, and refresh himself for the labours of the day.

Few lads could have been more insensible to the impressions of a life thus passed among the ensigns of mortality. His mind was closed against all general considerations. He was incapable of interest in the fate and fortunes of another, the slave of his own desires and low ambitions. Cold, light, and selfish in the last resort, he had that modicum of prudence, miscalled morality, which keeps a man from inconvenient drunkenness or punishable theft. He coveted, besides, a measure of consideration from his masters and his fellow-pupils, and he had no desire to fail conspicuously in the external parts of life. Thus he made it his pleasure to gain some distinction in his studies, and day after day rendered unimpeachable eye-service to his employer, Mr K—. For his day of work he indemnified himself by nights of roaring, blackguardly enjoyment; and when that balance had been struck, the organ that he called his conscience declared itself content.

The supply of subjects was a continual trouble to him as well as to his master. In that large and busy class, the raw material of the anatomists kept perpetually running out; and the business thus rendered necessary was not only unpleasant in itself, but threatened dangerous consequences to all who were concerned. It was the policy of Mr K— to ask no questions in his dealings with the trade. 'They bring the body, and we pay the price,' he used to say, dwelling on the alliteration – '*quid pro quo*.' And again, and somewhat profanely, 'Ask no questions,' he would tell his assistants, 'for conscience sake.' There was no understanding that the subjects were provided by the crime of murder. Had that idea been broached to him in words, he would have recoiled in horror; but the lightness of his speech upon so grave a matter was, in itself, an offence against good manners, and a temptation to the men with whom he dealt. Fettes, for instance, had often remarked to himself upon the singular freshness of the bodies. He had been struck again and again by the hang-dog, abominable looks of the ruffians who came to him before the dawn; and putting things together clearly in his private thoughts, he perhaps attributed a meaning too immoral and too categorical to the unguarded counsels of his master. He understood his duty, in short, to have three branches: to take what was brought, to pay the price, and to avert the eye from any evidence of crime.

One November morning this policy of silence was put sharply to the test. He had been awake all night with a racking toothache – pacing his room like a caged beast or throwing himself in fury on his bed – and had fallen at last into that profound, uneasy slumber that so often follows on a night of pain, when he was awakened by the third or fourth angry repetition of the concerted signal. There was a thin, bright moonshine; it was bitter cold, windy, and frosty; the town had not yet awakened, but an indefinable stir already preluded the noise and business of the day. The ghouls had come later than usual, and they seemed more than usually eager to be gone. Fettes, sick with sleep, lighted them upstairs. He heard their grumbling Irish voices through a dream; and as they stripped the sack from their sad merchandise he leaned dozing, with his shoulder propped against the wall; he had to shake himself to find the men their money. As he did so his eyes lighted on the dead face. He started; he took two steps nearer, with the candle raised.

'God Almighty!' he cried. 'That is Jane Galbraith!' The men answered nothing, but they shuffled nearer the door.

'I know her, I tell you,' he continued. 'She was alive and hearty yesterday. It's impossible she can be dead; it's impossible you should have got this body fairly.'

'Sure, sir, you're mistaken entirely,' said one of the men.

But the other looked Fettes darkly in the eyes, and demanded the money on the spot.

It was impossible to misconceive the threat or to exaggerate the danger. The lad's heart failed him. He stammered some excuses, counted out the sum, and saw his hateful visitors depart. No sooner were they gone than he hastened to confirm his doubts. By a dozen unquestionable marks he identified the girl he had jested with the day before. He saw, with horror, marks upon her body that might well betoken violence. A panic seized him, and he took refuge in his room. There he reflected at length over the discovery that he had made; considered soberly the bearing of Mr K—'s instructions and the danger to himself of interference in so serious a business, and at last, in sore perplexity, determined to wait for the advice of his immediate superior, the class assistant.

This was a young doctor, Wolfe Macfarlane, a high favourite among all the reckless students, clever, dissipated, and unscrupulous to the last degree. He had travelled and studied abroad. His manners were agreeable and a little forward. He was an authority on the stage, skilful on the ice or the links with skate or golf-club; he dressed with nice audacity, and, to put the finishing touch upon his glory, he kept a gig and a strong trotting-horse. With Fettes he was on terms of intimacy; indeed, their relative positions called for some community of life; and when subjects were scarce the pair would drive far into the country in Macfarlane's gig, visit and desecrate some lonely graveyard, and return before dawn with their booty to the door of the dissecting-room.

On that particular morning Macfarlane arrived somewhat earlier than his wont. Fettes heard him, and met him on the stairs, told him his story, and showed him the cause of his alarm. Macfarlane examined the marks on her body.

'Yes,' he said with a nod, 'it looks fishy.'

'Well, what should I do?,' asked Fettes.

'Do?' repeated the other. 'Do you want to do anything? Least said soonest mended, I should say.'

'Some one else might recognise her,' objected Fettes. 'She was as well known as the Castle Rock.'

'We'll hope not,' said Macfarlane, 'and if anybody does – well, you didn't, don't you see, and there's an end. The fact is, this has been going on too long. Stir up the mud, and you'll get K— into the most unholy trouble; you'll be in a shocking box yourself. So will I, if you come to that. I should like to know how any one of us would look, or what the devil we should have to say for ourselves in any Christian witness-box. For me, you know there's one thing certain – that, practically speaking, all our subjects have been murdered.'

'Macfarlane!' cried Fettes.

'Come now!' sneered the other. 'As if you hadn't suspected it yourself!'

'Suspecting is one thing——.'

'And proof another. Yes, I know; and I'm as sorry as you are this should have come here,' tapping the body with his cane. 'The next best thing for me is not to recognise it; and,' he added coolly, 'I don't. You may, if you please. I don't dictate, but I think a man of the world would do as I do; and I may add, I fancy that is what K— would look for at our hands. The question is, Why did he choose us two for his assistants? And I answer, because he didn't want old wives.'

This was the tone of all others to affect the mind of a lad like Fettes. He agreed to imitate Macfarlane. The body of the unfortunate girl was duly dissected, and no one remarked or appeared to recognize her.

One afternoon, when his day's work was over, Fettes dropped into a popular tavern and found Macfarlane sitting with a stranger. This was a small man, very pale and dark, with coal-black eyes. The cut of his features gave a promise of intellect and refinement which was but feebly realised in his manners, for he proved, upon a nearer acquaintance, coarse, vulgar, and stupid. He exercised, however, a very remarkable control over Macfarlane; issued orders like the Great Bashaw; became inflamed at the least discussion or delay, and commented rudely on the servility with which he was obeyed. This most offensive person took a fancy to Fettes on the spot, plied him with drinks, and honoured him with unusual confidences on his past career. If a tenth part of what he confessed were true, he was a very loathsome rogue; and the lad's vanity was tickled by the attention of so experienced a man.

'I'm a pretty bad fellow myself,' the stranger remarked, 'but Macfarlane is the boy – Toddy Macfarlane, I call him. Toddy, order your friend another glass.' Or it might be, 'Toddy, you jump up and shut the door.' 'Toddy hates me,' he said again. 'Oh, yes, Toddy, you do!'

'Don't you call me that confounded name,' growled Macfarlane.

'Hear him! Did you ever see the lads play knife? He would like to do that all over my body,' remarked the stranger.

'We medicals have a better way than that,' said Fettes. 'When we dislike a dead friend of ours, we dissect him.'

Macfarlane looked up sharply, as though this jest was scarcely to his mind.

The afternoon passed. Gray, for that was the stranger's name, invited Fettes to join them at dinner, ordered a feast so sumptuous that the tavern was thrown in commotion, and when all was done commanded Macfarlane to settle the bill. It was late before they separated; the man Gray was incapably drunk. Macfarlane, sobered by his fury, chewed the cud of the money he had been forced to squander and the slights he had been obliged to swallow. Fettes, with various liquors singing in his head, returned home with devious footsteps and a mind entirely in abeyance. Next day Macfarlane was absent from the class, and Fettes smiled to himself as he imagined him still squiring the intolerable Gray from tavern to tavern. As soon as the hour of liberty had struck he posted from place to place in quest of his last night's companions. He could find them, however, nowhere; so returned early to his rooms, went early to bed, and slept the sleep of the just.

At four in the morning he was awakened by the well-known signal. Descending to the door, he was filled with astonishment to find Macfarlane with his gig, and in the gig one of those long and ghastly packages with which he was so well acquainted.

'What?' he cried. 'Have you been out alone? How did you manage?'

But Macfarlane silenced him roughly, bidding him turn to business. When they had got the body upstairs and laid it on the table, Macfarlane made at first as if he were going away. Then he paused and seemed to hesitate; and then, 'You had better look at the face,' said he, in tones of some constraint. 'You had better,' he repeated, as Fettes only stared at him in wonder.

'But where, and how, and when did you come by it?' cried the other.

'Look at the face,' was the only answer.

Fettes was staggered; strange doubts assailed him. He looked from the young doctor to the body, and then back again. At last, with a start, he did as he was bidden. He had almost expected the sight that met his eyes, and yet the shock was cruel. To see, fixed in the rigidity of death and naked on that coarse layer of sackcloth, the man whom he had left well clad and full of meat and sin upon the threshold of a tavern, awoke, even in the thoughtless Fettes, some of the terrors of the conscience. It was a *cras tibi* which re-echoed in his soul, that two whom he had known should have come to lie upon these icy tables. Yet these were only secondary thoughts. His first concern regarded Wolfe. Unprepared for a challenge so momentous, he knew not how to look his comrade in the face. He durst not meet his eye, and he had neither words nor voice at his command.

It was Macfarlane himself who made the first advance. He came up quietly behind and laid his hand gently but firmly on the other's shoulder.

'Richardson,' said he, 'may have the head.'

Now Richardson was a student who had long been anxious for that portion of the human subject to dissect. There was no answer, and the murderer resumed: 'Talking of business, you must pay me; your accounts, you see, must tally.'

Fettes found a voice, the ghost of his own: 'Pay you!' he cried. 'Pay you for that?'

'Why, yes, of course you must. By all means and on every possible account, you must,' returned the other. 'I dare not give it for nothing, you dare not take it for nothing; it would compromise us both. This is another case like Jane Galbraith's. The more things are wrong the more we must act as if all were right. Where does old K— keep his money?'

'There,' answered Fettes hoarsely, pointing to a cupboard in the corner.

'Give me the key, then,' said the other, calmly, holding out his hand.

There was an instant's hesitation, and the die was cast. Macfarlane could not suppress a nervous twitch, the infinitesimal mark of an immense relief, as he felt the key between his fingers. He opened the cupboard, brought out pen and ink and a paper-book that stood in one compartment, and separated from the funds in a drawer a sum suitable to the occasion.

'Now, look here,' he said, 'there is the payment made – first proof of your good faith: first step to your security. You have now to clinch it by a second. Enter the payment in your book, and then you for your part may defy the devil.'

The next few seconds were for Fettes an agony of thought; but in balancing his terrors it was the most immediate that triumphed. Any future difficulty seemed almost welcome if he could avoid a present quarrel with Macfarlane. He set down the candle which he had been carrying all this time, and with a steady hand entered the date, the nature, and the amount of the transaction.

'And now,' said Macfarlane, 'it's only fair that you should pocket the lucre. I've had my share already. By the bye, when a man of the world falls into a bit of luck, has a few shillings extra in his pocket – I'm ashamed to speak of it, but there's a rule of conduct in the case. No treating, no purchase of expensive class-books, no squaring of old debts; borrow, don't lend.'

'Macfarlane,' began Fettes, still somewhat hoarsely, 'I have put my neck in a halter to oblige you.'

'To oblige me?' cried Wolfe. 'Oh, come! You did, as near as I can see the matter, what you downright had to do in self-defence. Suppose I got into trouble, where would you be? This second little matter flows clearly from the first. Mr Gray is the continuation of Miss Galbraith. You can't begin and then stop. If you begin, you must keep on beginning; that's the truth. No rest for the wicked.'

A horrible sense of blackness and the treachery of fate seized hold upon the soul of the unhappy student.

'My God!' he cried, 'but what have I done? and when did I begin? To be made a class assistant – in the name of reason, where's the harm in that? Service wanted the position; Service might have got it. Would he have been where I am now?'

'My dear fellow,' said Macfarlane, 'what a boy you are! What harm has come to you? What harm can come to you if you hold your tongue? Why, man, do you know what this life is? There are two squads of us – the lions, and the lambs. If you're a lamb, you'll come to lie upon these tables like Gray or Jane Galbraith; if you're a lion, you'll live and drive a horse like me, like K—, like all the world with any wit or courage. You're staggered at the first. But look at K—! My dear fellow, you're clever, you have pluck. I like you, and K— likes you. You were born to lead the hunt; and I tell you, on my honour and my experience of life, three days from now you'll laugh at all these scarecrows like a high-school boy at a farce.'

And with that Macfarlane took his departure and drove off up the wynd in his gig to get under cover before daylight. Fettes was thus left alone with his regrets. He saw the miserable peril in which he stood involved. He saw, with inexpressible dismay, that there was no limit to his weakness, and that, from concession to concession, he had fallen from the arbiter of Macfarlane's destiny to his paid and helpless accomplice. He would have given the world to have been a little braver at the time, but it did not occur to him that he might still be brave. The secret of Jane Galbraith and the cursed entry in the daybook closed his mouth.

Hours passed; the class began to arrive; the members of the unhappy Gray were dealt out to one and to another, and received without remark. Richardson was made happy with the head; and before the hour of freedom rang Fettes trembled with exultation to perceive how far they had already gone toward safety.

For two days he continued to watch, with increasing joy, the dreadful process of disguise.

On the third day Macfarlane made his appearance. He had been ill, he said; but he made up for lost time by the energy with which he directed the students. To Richardson in particular he extended the most valuable assistance and advice, and that student, encouraged by the praise of the demonstrator, burned high with ambitious hopes, and saw the medal already in his grasp.

Before the week was out Macfarlane's prophecy had been fulfilled. Fettes had outlived his terrors and had forgotten his baseness. He began to plume himself upon his courage, and had so arranged the story in his mind that he could look back on these events with an unhealthy pride. Of his accomplice he saw but little. They met, of course, in the business of the class; they received their orders together from Mr K—. At times they had a word or two in private, and Macfarlane was from first to last particularly kind and jovial. But it was plain that he avoided any reference to their common secret; and even when Fettes whispered to him that he had cast in his lot with the lions and forsworn the lambs, he only signed to him smilingly to hold his peace.

At length an occasion arose which threw the pair once more into a closer union. Mr K— was again short of subjects; pupils were eager, and it was a part of this teacher's pretensions to be always well supplied. At the same time there came the news of a burial in the rustic graveyard of Glencorse. Time has little changed the place in question. It stood then, as now, upon a cross road, out of call of human habitations, and buried fathoms deep in the foliage of six cedar trees. The cries of the sheep upon the neighbouring hills, the streamlets upon either hand, one loudly singing among pebbles, the other dripping furtively from pond to pond, the stir of the wind in mountainous old flowering chestnuts, and once in seven days the voice of the bell and the old tunes of the precentor, were the only sounds that disturbed the silence around the rural church. The Resurrection Man – to use a byname of the period – was not to be deterred by any of the sanctities of customary piety. It was part of his trade to despise and desecrate the scrolls and trumpets of old tombs, the paths worn by the feet of worshippers and mourners, and the offerings and the inscriptions of bereaved affection. To rustic neighbour-hoods, where love is more than commonly tenacious, and where some bonds of blood or fellowship unite the entire society of a parish, the body-snatcher, far from being repelled by natural respect, was attracted by the ease and safety of the task. To bodies that had been laid in earth, in joyful expectation of a far different awakening, there came that hasty, lamp-lit, terror-haunted resurrection of the spade and mattock. The coffin was forced, the cerements torn, and the melancholy relics, clad in sackcloth, after being rattled for hours on moonless byways, were at length exposed to uttermost indignities before a class of gaping boys.

Somewhat as two vultures may swoop upon a dying lamb, Fettes and Macfarlane were to be let loose upon a grave in that green and quiet resting-place. The wife of a farmer, a woman who had lived for sixty years, and been known for nothing but good butter and a godly conversation, was to be rooted from her grave at midnight and carried, dead and naked to that far-away city that she had always honoured with her Sunday's best; the place beside her family was to be empty till the crack of doom; her innocent and almost venerable members to be exposed to that last curiosity of the anatomist.

Late one afternoon the pair set forth, well wrapped in cloaks and furnished with a formidable bottle. It rained without remission – a cold, dense, lashing rain. Now and again there blew a puff of wind, but these sheets of falling water kept it down. Bottle and all, it was a sad and silent drive as far as Penicuik, where they were to spend the evening. They stopped once, to hide their implements in a thick bush not far from the churchyard, and once again at the Fisher's Tryst, to have a toast before the kitchen fire and vary their nips of whisky with a glass of ale. When they reached their journey's end the gig was housed, the horse was fed and comforted, and the two young doctors in a private room sat down to the best dinner and the best wine the house afforded. The lights, the fire, the beating rain upon the window, the cold, incongruous work that lay before them, added zest to their enjoyment of the meal. With every glass their cordiality increased. Soon Macfarlane handed a little pile of gold to his companion.

'A compliment,' he said. 'Between friends these little d——d accommodations ought to fly like pipe-lights.'

Fettes pocketed the money, and applauded the sentiment to the echo. 'You are a philosopher,' he cried. 'I was an ass till I knew you. You and K— between you, by the Lord Harry! but you'll make a man of me.'

'Of course, we shall,' applauded Macfarlane. 'A man? I tell you, it required a man to back me up the other morning. There are some big, brawling, forty-year-old cowards who would have turned sick at the look of the d——d thing; but not you – you kept your head. I watched you.'

'Well, and why not?' Fettes thus vaunted himself.

'It was no affair of mine. There was nothing to gain on the one side but disturbance, and on the other I could count on your gratitude, don't you see?' And he slapped his pocket till the gold pieces rang.

Macfarlane somehow felt a certain touch of alarm at these unpleasant words. He may have regretted that he had taught his young companion so successfully, but he had no time to interfere, for the other noisily continued in this boastful strain:

'The great thing is not to be afraid. Now, between you and me, I don't want to hang – that's practical; but for all cant, Macfarlane, I was born with a contempt. Hell, God, Devil, right, wrong, sin, crime, and all the old gallery of curiosities – they may frighten boys, but men of the world, like you and me, despise them. Here's to the memory of Gray!'

It was by this time growing somewhat late. The gig, according to order, was brought round to the door with both lamps brightly shining, and the young men had to pay their bill and take the road. They announced that they were bound for Peebles, and drove in that direction till they were clear of the last houses of the town; then, extinguishing the lamps, returned upon their course, and followed a by-road toward Glencorse. There was no sound but that of their own passage, and the incessant, strident pouring of the rain. It was pitch dark; here and there a white gate or a white stone in the wall guided them for a short space across the night; but for the most part it was at a foot pace, and almost groping, that they picked their way through that resonant blackness to their solemn and isolated destination. In the sunken woods that traverse the neighbourhood of the burying-ground the last glimmer failed them, and it became necessary to kindle a match and reillumine one of the lanterns of the gig. Thus, under the dripping trees, and environed by huge and moving shadows, they reached the scene of their unhallowed labours.

They were both experienced in such affairs, and powerful with the spade; and they had scarce been twenty minutes at their task before they were rewarded by a dull rattle on the coffin lid. At the same moment Macfarlane, having hurt his hand upon a stone, flung it carelessly above his head. The grave, in which they now stood almost to the shoulders, was close to the edge of the plateau of the graveyard; and the gig lamp had been propped, the better to illuminate their labours, against a tree, and on the immediate verge of the steep bank descending to the stream. Chance had taken a sure aim with the stone. Then came a clang of broken glass; night fell upon them; sounds alternately dull and ringing announced the bounding of the lantern down the bank, and its occasional collision with the trees. A stone or two, which it had dislodged in its descent, rattled behind it into the profundities of the glen; and then silence, like night, resumed its sway; and they might bend their hearing to its utmost pitch, but naught was to be heard except the rain, now marching to the wind, now steadily falling over miles of open country.

They were so nearly at an end of their abhorred task that they judged it wisest to complete it in the dark. The coffin was exhumed and broken open; the body inserted in the dripping sack and carried between them to the gig; one mounted to keep it in its place, and the other, taking the horse by the mouth, groped along by wall and bush until they reached the wider road by the Fisher's Tryst. Here was a faint, diffused radiancy, which they hailed like daylight; by that they pushed the horse to a good pace and began to rattle along merrily in the direction of the town.

They had both been wetted to the skin during their operations, and now, as the gig jumped among the deep ruts, the thing that stood propped between them fell now upon one and now upon the other. At every repetition of the horrid contact each instinctively repelled it with the greater haste; and the process, natural although it was, began to tell upon the nerves of the companions. Macfarlane made some ill-favoured jest about the farmer's wife, but it came hollowly from his lips, and was allowed to drop in silence. Still their unnatural burden bumped from side to side; and now the head would be laid, as if in confidence, upon their shoulders, and now the drenching sackcloth would flap icily about their faces. A creeping chill began to possess the soul of Fettes. He peered at the bundle, and it seemed somehow larger than at first. All over the countryside, and from every degree of distance, the farm dogs accompanied their passage with tragic ululations; and it grew and grew upon his mind that some unnatural miracle had been accomplished, that some nameless change had befallen the dead body, and that it was in fear of their unholy burden that the dogs were howling.

'For God's sake,' said he, making a great effort to arrive at speech, 'for God's sake, let's have a light!'

Seemingly Macfarlane was affected in the same direction; for, though he made no reply, he stopped the horse, passed the reins to his companion, got down, and proceeded to kindle the remaining lamp. They had by that time got no farther than the cross-road down to Auchenclinny. The rain still poured as though the deluge were returning, and it was no easy matter to make a light in such a world of wet and darkness. When at last the flickering blue flame had been transferred to the wick and began to expand and clarify, and shed a wide circle of misty brightness round the gig, it became possible for the two young men to see each other and the thing they had along with them. The rain had moulded the rough sacking to the outlines of the body underneath; the head was distinct from the trunk, the shoulders plainly modelled; something at once spectral and human riveted their eyes upon the ghastly comrade of their drive.

For some time Macfarlane stood motionless, holding up the lamp. A nameless dread was swathed, like a wet sheet, about the body, and tightened the white skin upon the face of Fettes; a fear that was meaningless, a horror of what could not be, kept mounting to his brain. Another beat of the watch, and he had spoken. But his comrade forestalled him.

'That is not a woman,' said Macfarlane in a hushed voice.

'It was a woman when we put her in,' whispered Fettes.

'Hold that lamp,' said the other. 'I must see her face.'

And as Fettes took the lamp his companion untied the fastenings of the sack and drew down the cover from the head. The light fell very clear upon the dark, well-moulded features and smooth-shaven cheeks of a too familiar countenance, often beheld in dreams of both of these young men. A wild yell rang up into the night; each leaped from his own side into the roadway; the lamp fell, broke and was extinguished; and the horse, terrified by this unusual commotion, bounded and went off toward Edinburgh at a gallop, bearing along with it, sole occupant of the gig, the body of the dead and long-dissected Gray.

SELECT BIBLIOGRAPHY

General (Including Burke & Hare)

Adams, Norman *Dead and Buried? The Horrible History of Bodysnatching* (Bell Publishing; New York, 1972)

—— *Scottish Bodysnatchers: True Accounts* (Goblinshead; Musselburgh, 2002)

Bailey, Brian *The Resurrection Men: A History of the Trade in Corpses* (Macdonald; London, 1991)

—— *Burke and Hare: The Year of the Ghouls* (Mainstream Publishing; Edinburgh & London, 2002)

Bailey, James Blake *The Diary of a Resurrectionist 1811-1812* (Swan Sonnenschein & Co.; London, 1896)

Brandon, David and Alan Brooke *London City of the Dead* (The History Press; Stroud, 2008)

Burch, Druin *Digging Up The Dead* (Chatto & Windus; London, 2007)

Chambers, Robert *Domestic Annals of Scotland from the Reformation to the Revolution* (W. & R. Chambers; Edinburgh & London, 1859)

Cohen, Daniel *The Body Snatchers* (J. M. Dent & Sons; London, 1977)

Comrie, John D. *History of Scottish Medicine to 1860* (The Wellcome Historical Medical Museum; London, 1927)

Douglas, Hugh *Burke and Hare: The True Story* (Robert Hale; London, 1973)

Edwards, Owen Dudley *Burke & Hare* (The Mercat Press; Edinburgh, 1993)

Fido, Martin *Bodysnatchers: A History of the Resurrectionists 1742-1832* (Weidenfield & Nicolson; London, 1988)

Gordon, Anne *Death is for the Living* (Paul Harris Publishing; Edinburgh, 1984)

Hone, William *The Every-Day Book and Table Book* (Thomas Tegg; London, 1827)

Knight, Alanna *Burke & Hare* (The National Archives; Richmond, 2007)

—— *The Robert Louis Stevenson Treasury* (Shepheard-Walwyn, London, 1985)

Livingstone, Sheila *Confess and Be Hanged: Scottish Crime & Punishment Through the Ages* (Birlinn; Edinburgh, 2000)

Lonsdale, Henry *A Sketch of the Life and Writings of Robert Knox, the Anatomist* (Macmillan & Co.; London, 1870)

Love, Dane *Scottish Kirkyards* (Robert Hale; London, 1989)

MacGregor, George *The History of Burke and Hare and of the Resurrectionist Times: A Fragment from the Criminal Annals of Scotland* (Thomas D. Morison; Glasgow & Hamilton, Adams, & Co.; London, 1884)

Richardson, Ruth *Death, Dissection and the Destitute* (Penguin; London, 1989)

Rosner, Lisa *The Anatomy Murders* (University of Pennsylvania Press; Philadelphia, 2010)

Roughead, William *Notable British Trials: Burke and Hare* (William Hodge & Co.; London, Edinburgh & Glasgow, 1921)

Section One: Edinburgh And The Lothians

Baird, William *Annals of Duddingston and Portobello* (Andrew Elliot; Edinburgh, 1898)

Blades, Daniel and Jean *Fala and Soutra: Past and Present* (Edinburgh, 1987)

Bookman Extra Number 'Robert Louis Stevenson' (Hodder & Stoughton; London, 1913)

Carrick, J.C. *The Abbey of St Mary Newbattle* (George Lewis & Co.; Selkirk & John Menzies & Co.; Edinburgh; 1908)

Lawrie, Archibald *The Psychic Investigators Casebook Volume Two* (AuthorHouse; Bloomington, Indiana, 2005)

McNeil, Peter *Tranent and its Surroundings* (J. Menzies & Co.; Edinburgh, 1883)

Moir, David Macbeth *The Life of Mansie Wauch, Tailor in Dalkeith. Written By Himself* (Collins & Hannay, *et al*; Philadelphia, 1828)

Montgomery, George *A History of Newton Parish* (George Montgomery; 1984)

Primrose, James *Strathbrock or the History and Antiquities of the Parish of Uphall* (Andrew Elliot; Edinburgh, 1898)

Ramsey, Ted *Don't Walk Down College Street* (Ramshorn; Glasgow, 1985)

Watt, Francis *The Book of Edinburgh Anecdote* (T.N. Foulis; London & Edinburgh, 1913)

West Lothian Local History Library *Grave Robbers in West Lothian* (West Lothian Libraries; Blackburn, 2002)

Wilson, John J. *Annals of Penicuik, Being a History of the Parish and of the Village* (T. & A. Constable; Penicuik, 1891)

Section Two: Glasgow And The West

Anon 'Supposed Murder' broadsheet in National Library of Scotland, shelfmark F.3.a.13(34) (1827)

Adamson, Archibald R. *Rambles Round Kilmarnock* (T. Stevenson, 'Standard' Office; Kilmarnock, 1875)

Aird, Andrew *Glimpses of Old Glasgow* (Aird & Coghill; Glasgow, 1894)

Alison, Robert *The Anecdotage of Glasgow* (Morison; Glasgow, 1892)

Berry, James J. *The Glasgow Necropolis: Heritage Trail and Historical Account* (City of Glasgow District Council; Glasgow, 1985)

Brown, Robert *The History of Paisley* (J. & J. Cook; Paisley, 1886)

Callant, A.G. *Saint Mungo's Bells; Or Old Glasgow Stories Rung Out Anew* (David Bryce; Glasgow, 1888)

Cant, Ronald G. and Ian G. Lindsay *Old Glasgow* (Oliver & Boyd; Edinburgh, 1947)

Cleland, James *Annals of Glasgow* (James Hedderwick/The Glasgow Royal Infirmary; Glasgow, 1816)

Coutts, James *A History of the University of Glasgow From its Foundation in 1451 to 1909* (James Maclehose & Sons; Glasgow, 1909)

Craufurd, George *The History of the Shire of Renfrew* (Alex. Weir; Paisley, 1782)

Glenday, David *Anderston As It Was* (Glasgow City Libraries; Glasgow, 1994)

Gray, James T. *Maybole, Carrick's Capital Facts, Fiction & Folks* (Alloway Publishing; Ayr, 1972)

House, Jack *The Heart of Glasgow* (Richard Drew Publishing; Glasgow, 1972)

Howie, James *An Historical Account of The Town of Ayr for the Last Fifty Years* (James McKie; Kilmarnock, 1861)

Johnston, Ruth *Glasgow Necropolis Afterlives: Tales of Interments* (Johnstonedesign; Glasgow, 2007)

Kenna, Rudolph and Ian Sutherland *They Belonged to Glasgow: the city from the bottom up* (Neil Wilson Publishing; Glasgow, 2001)

MacDonald, Hugh *Rambles Round Glasgow: Descriptive, Historical and Traditional* (John Smith & Son; Glasgow, 1910. Originally published 1854)

McKenzie Peter *Reminiscences of Glasgow and the West of Scotland* (John Tweed; Glasgow, 1865-68)

McClelland, Robert *The Church & Parish of Inchinnan: A Brief History* (Alexander Gardner; Paisley, 1905)

Mort, Frederick *Renfrewshire* (Cambridge University Press; Cambridge, 1919)

Scott, Ronnie *Death by Design: The True Story of the Glasgow Necropolis* (Black & White Publishing; Edinburgh, 2005)

Thomson, Alexander *Random Notes and Rambling Recollections of Drydock, the Dock, or Kelvindock, all Now Known by the More Modern Name of Maryhill: 1750-1894* (Kerr & Richardson; Glasgow, 1894)

Section Three: Southern Scotland

Bradley, A.G. *The Gateway of Scotland: or, East Lothian, Lammermoor and the Merse* (Constable & Co.; London, 1912)

Brown, James *The History of Sanquhar* (J. Anderson & Son; Dumfries, 1891)

Eyre-Todd, George *Byways of the Scottish Border* (James Lewis; Selkirk, 1893)

Lang, Andrew and John Lang *Highways and Byways in the Border* (Macmillan & Co.; London, 1914)

Lang, Jean *North and South of Tweed: Stories and Legends of the Borders* (T.C. & E.C. Jack; London, 1913)

Williamson, Alex. *Glimpses of Peebles, Or, Forgotten Chapters in its History* (George Lewis; Edinburgh & Selkirk; 1895)

Wilson, William *Folk Lore and Genealogies of Uppermost Nithsdale* (Robert G. Mann; Dumfries, 1904)

Section Four: The Forth Valley

Anon 'Riot in Stirling', broadside in National Library of Scotland, shelfmark Ry.III.a.2(35), 1823

Barty, James Webster 'Kirk Session Records' in *Bulletin of The Society of Friends of Dunblane Cathedral* Vol. VI, Part IV 1953

Caird, Janet *The Umbrella-Maker's Daughter* (MacMillan; London, 1980)

Drysdale, William *Old Faces, Old Places and Old Stories of Stirling* (Eneas Mackay; Stirling, 1898)

MacKay, Moray S. *Doune: Historical Notes (Notes on the Parish of Kilmadock and Borough of Doune)* (Forth Naturalist and Historian Editorial Board; Stirling, 1984, first printed privately 1953)

Nimmo, William *The History of Stirlingshire* (Hamilton, Adams & Co.; London, 1880)

Salmon, Thomas James *Borrowstounness and District, Being Historical Sketches of Kinneil, Carriden, and Bo'ness c. 1550-1850* (William Hodge & Co.; Edinburgh & London, 1913)

Stirling Council Libraries *Stirling's Talking Stones* (Stirling Council Libraries; Stirling, 2002)

Section Five: East Central Scotland

Anon *Dundee and Dundonians Seventy Years Ago: Being Personal Reminiscences of an Old Dundonian* (James P. Mathew & Co.; Dundee, 1892)

Beatts, J.M. *Reminiscences of a Dundonian* (George Petrie; Dundee, 1882)

Buchanan, Dr G. 'Reminiscences of Body Lifting' in unnamed newspaper, *c.* 1867 (Item 250 in *Perth Pamphlets* Vol 12, in the A.K. Bell Library, Perth)

Gourlay, George *Our Old Neighbours; Or, Folk Lore of the East of Fife* (D.C. Thomson; Dundee, 1887)

Haggarty, George and Nicholas Reynolds 'Recent excavations at Dunfermline Abbey, Fife' in *Proceedings of the Society of Antiquaries in Scotland*, Vol. 111 (1981)

Lamb, A.C. *Dundee: Its Quaint and Historic Buildings* (George Petrie; Dundee, 1895)

Marshall, William *Historic Scenes in Perthshire* (William Oliphant & Co.; Edinburgh, 1879)

Penny, George *Traditions of Perth* (Dewar, Sidey, Morison, Peat and Drummond; Perth, 1836 – reprinted Wm Culross & Son; Coupar Angus, 1986)

Reid, Alan 'Churchyard memorials of St Andrew's' in *Proceedings of the Society of Antiquaries in Scotland*, Vol. 45 (1911)

Wilson, John Mackay *Wilson's Historical, Traditionary, and Imaginative Tales of the Borders, and of Scotland* Vol. 6. (William Mackenzie; London, 1877)

Section Six: The North-East

Anon. 'A New Way of Raising the Wind!' (1829), broadside in National Library of Scotland, shelfmark: Ry.III.a.6(047)

Anon. 'Burking Shop Destroyed' (1831), broadside in National Library of Scotland, shelfmark: F.3.a.13(6)

Gregor, Walter 'Notes and Queries: Unspoken Nettles' in *The Folk-Lore Journal*, Vol. 2, No. 12 (Dec., 1884)

Henderson, John A. *History of The Parish of Banchory-Devenick* (D. Wyllie & Son; Aberdeen, 1890)

—— *Annals of Lower Deeside, Being a Topographical, Proprietary, Ecclesiastical, and Antiquarian History of Durris, Drumoak, and Culter* (D. Wyllie & Son; Aberdeen, 1892)

Ritchie, James 'An Account of the Watch-Houses, Mortsafes, and Public Vaults in Aberdeenshire Churchyards, Formerly Used for the Protection of the Dead from The Resurrectionists' in *Proceedings of the Society of Antiquaries in Scotland*, Vol. 46 (1911-12)

——"Relics Of The Body-Snatchers: Supplementary Notes On Mortsafe Tackle, Mortsafes, Watch-Houses, and Public Vaults, Mostly in Aberdeenshire" in *Proceedings of the Society of Antiquaries in Scotland*, Vol. 55 (1920-21)

Rorie, David 'Stray Notes on the Folk-Lore of Aberdeenshire and the North-East of Scotland' in *Folklore*, Vol. 25, No. 3 (Sep. 30, 1914)

Smith, Robert *The Hidden City: The Story of Aberdeen and its People* (John Donald; Edinburgh, 1999)

Stewart, James *Deeside Tinkers* (McKenzie Quality Print; Dyce, 2007)

Thomson, James *Recollections of a Speyside Parish* (The Moray and Nairn Newspaper Co.; Elgin, 1902)

Rodger, Ella Hill Burton *Aberdeen Doctors at Home and Abroad: The Narrative of a Medical School* (William Blackwood & Sons; Edinburgh & London, 1893)

Section Seven: The North And West Highlands

Inverness Museum & Art Gallery *Graveyards Old and New in Inverness District* (Inverness, n.d.)

Longmore, Leonella *Inverness in the 18th Century* (Courier Publications; Inverness, 2001)

MacDonald, Alexander *Story and Song from Loch Ness-Side* (Northern Counties Newspaper and Printing and Publishing Co.; Inverness, 1914)

INDEX

PERSONS

STRUCTURES/ ARTEFACTS